THINK
The Road Less Traveled

Scott Burgmeyer

&

Tammy K. Rogers

Copyright © 2025 Scott Burgmeyer & Tammy K. Rogers

Published by: Happy Jack Editing and Publishing

All rights reserved.

No part of this publication may be reproduced, stored in a retrieval system, or transmitted in any form without prior written permission of the publisher. The only exception is brief quotations in printed reviews.

Images created by OpenAI ChatGPT

This book is a summary of research and experience. Any resemblance to actual persons, living or dead, or events are coincidental.

ISBN: 978-1-944104-39-9

DEDICATION

This book is dedicated to all of those who love to think—past, present, and future.

CONTENTS

Introduction: Our Thinking Is About As Deep as a Parking Lot Puddle — 1

PART 1: **The Need for Thinking** — 15

1. How Shallow Thinking Crushed Precise Manufacturing — 17
2. We're Too Busy to Think About This $hit — 27
3. The Power of Thinking — 47
4. The Mind Games We Play — 53

PART 2: **The ROADD to Deeper Thinking** — 65

5. Getting on the ROADD — 67

PART 3: **Cultivating a Culture of Thinking** — 89

6. Organizational Thinking Tactic 1: The Growth Questions — 99
7. Organizational Thinking Tactic 2: Stay Stupid Longer (SSL) — 115
8. Organizational Thinking Tactic 3: Readers Are Thinkers — 125
9. Organizational Thinking Tactic 4: Carve Out Thinking Time — 137
10. Organizational Thinking Tactic 5: Expand Facilitation & Problem Solving — 153

| 11 | Organizational Thinking Tactic 6: Lead Them Down the ROADD | 159 |

Conclusion 169

References 179

THINK

ACKNOWLEDGMENTS

Michael, Beth, Ben & Josh — Thanks for your love and understanding when we spent time away from you to create this. Your support has allowed us to work with others to become more together.

Introduction
Our Thinking Is About as Deep as a Parking Lot Puddle

1

THINK

We're drowning in information. Every last one of us.

News feeds, books, podcasts, emails, texts, social media ... they're all screaming for our attention. It's like trying to have a conversation at a rock concert. You can barely hear yourself think. And let's not even talk about the pressure to always be "on."

- Smart phones that demand to be answered.
- Client requests.
- Productivity expectations.
- Deadlines.

The sheer amount of information coming at us is more than overwhelming—and that's NOT even our biggest problem. The more important issue is how we interact and engage with all of this information.

These kinds of pressures and the constant barrage of distractions are turning us into shallow thinkers. We skim articles, rely on quick Google searches, use AI to get things done, and jump from one task to the next without ever really diving deeply into anything. It's a little bit like junk food. We're putting stuff in, and we're not getting what we need to build strength, muscles, or endurance.

As leadership and organizational consultants, we (Scott and Tammy) see how information overload has changed today's work force. Week after week, we encounter employees that have developed coping mechanisms for managing the onslaught of information. And unfortunately, most of these workarounds aren't serving the employees, leaders, or organizations very well.

Let's take a look at the common ways many of us deal with all of this information. Maybe you know, live with, or work alongside some of these personas.

Running Rodney

We bet you've met Rodney. Rodney is the employee who has been given an assignment and is already running at 600 mph before his boss even finishes talking about it.

- Questions? No.
- Dialogue? No.
- Thinking? No.

Taking the time to understand the bigger picture? Ain't nobody got time for that.

Why would Rodney waste time on any of that when there's a deadline to meet and a task to check off on his to-do list?

Let's Goooooo!!!

THINK

Echo Chamber Evelyn

Evelyn thrives in her own bubble in both her home and work life. She surrounds herself with people who share her opinions—creating an echo chamber where dissenting views are rarely heard.

Even the podcasts, television shows, articles, and books that she interacts with align with her world view.

While Evelyn may be well-informed, she only understands one side of the story.

THINK

Sound Bite Steve

Steve gets his information from soundbites and headlines, from skimming Slack group conversations, or from half-heard comments in the elevator.

Steve often forms opinions—strong opinions—based on this limited information. Which means he can't explain why he sees things this way, nor can he provide any background information or context for his opinions. He just has them.

Get Along Gary

When Gary's boss asks if he has any questions, Gary—who wants to prove his competence—usually says no.

Then Gary quickly gets to work without verifying his understanding or asking for clarification.

You see, Gary assumes that he has interpreted the instructions and information exactly how his boss sees it.

Gary is then surprised when his boss is unhappy with the work he turns in.

THINK

All-Knowing Alberto

Alberto KNOWS he is the smartest person in the room. He's read the book, researched the subject, and/or has done it before.

Alberto is known for interrupting others, dominating conversations, and dismissing other people's contributions.

Alberto believes there is one right answer—his. And his ego and over-confidence prevent him from seeing, seeking, and valuing diverse perspectives—which leads to strained relationships and missed opportunities.

Terry the Trend Follower

You know Terry. Terry jumps on every new fad, from extreme productivity hacks to the latest management buzzwords—often without fully understanding the underlying principles.

This has led to "flavor-of-the-month" solutions. Staff, initially intrigued by Terry's "forward-thinking" enthusiasm, have become frustrated as they are asked to implement the "newest and greatest initiative" without any consideration for sustainable work practices.

Jumping Julia

Julia leaps to conclusions with the speed of a gazelle and height of a kangaroo. One sentence into a conversation and Julia has already formed an opinion. Julia believes her logic leaps are correct—and more often than not Julia's assumptions are off-kilter.

Julia is filling in the blanks without verifying the accuracy of her thought patterns. And unfortunately, these logic leaps often lead Julia to believe that others are to blame or that others have ill intentions.

This bad habit has damaged Julia's reputation. Her colleagues don't trust her, don't think of her as a team player, and don't think she is smart and/or capable.

We're Moving, But Are We Getting Anywhere?
We're guessing that as you read about **Julia, Terry, Evelyn,** and the others you could see the faces of all the people in your life who NEED to read this book. If that's true, take a deep breath—because the person who needs to read this book is ... **YOU.**

It's easy to spot where OTHERS are reacting instead of thinking. It's much more difficult to see where YOU can improve your thinking. And if each of us were to honestly evaluate our own thinking, most of us would receive a failing grade.

(Said with just a bit of humor ...) **Think** about it for a minute. How often do you find yourself:

- Zoning out during a conversation, your mind drifting off to somewhere else?
- Scrolling through social media, mindlessly "consuming" information?
- Completing work without ever considering what good or excellent really looks like?

This "shallow thinking" isn't just a personal problem that leaves people feeling overwhelmed, anxious, and disconnected. It's hurting our organizations too. We're making rushed decisions, struggling to be innovative, and reacting to what is immediately in front of us—while we miss out on the bigger picture.

For many of us it feels like we're running—really f@#$ing fast—and still not getting anywhere.

So, what can we do?

How do we reclaim our ability to think deeply and truly engage with the world around us?

That's what we'll explore in the chapters to come.

First, let's take a closer look at why organizations and the people who work there should be concerned about shallow thinking (aka thinking as deep as a parking lot puddle).

THINK

Part 1
The Need for Thinking

1
How Shallow Thinking Crushed Precise Manufacturing

Precise Manufacturing—whose name has been changed to protect their identity—is a textbook example of a shallow-thinking organization. Once upon a time they were a productive, profitable, and preferred employer in Middle America.

Let us show you what we found when they called us in to consult ...

WHAT WE FOUND
Precise Manufacturing's Culture

Stifled Innovation
Precise Manufacturing used to be considered innovative. That, however, was long ago. Just consider the five phrases that the staff told us they

hear most often.

- That won't fit into our system.
- We've tried that before.
- That will create more problems than it solves.
- That's not who we are.
- Why fix something that isn't broken?

Silent Treatment
We also found that it's eerily quiet inside the walls of Precise Manufacturing. Yes—the machines are humming. But there's little to no face-to-face communication between staff. And don't even get us started on team meetings. They are downright uncomfortable. When managers ask for input and opinions, they are met with silence. Why? Behind closed doors the staff told us they believe that decisions have already been made, and that they are expected to "guess" and "align with" what their bosses have already decided. And if they don't? They assume, "Everything I say, can and will be used against me."

Whispers of Discontent
The little bit of conversation that IS happening between staff members often consists of hushed complaints about other people, other departments, and management decisions. And while some of these discussions are based in fact, the underlying issue is that the staff is concentrating on what is "wrong" with the organization instead of looking at what is "right"

with the organization.

Silos

Organization-wide trust and teamwork have taken a back seat to an individual and a departmental "me-and-mine" point of view. No one is really looking at or thinking through what is best for the organization and its customers. Most of the staff is simply concerned with their personal bonuses, and/or the department's numbers and metrics that impact their bonuses. And as a result, there is a lot of finger-pointing, blaming, and in-fighting. Which creates a culture of polarization and a scoreboard of winners and losers.

Subtle Sabotage

While the organization has not seen overt acts of rebellion, Precision Manufacturing employees have begun to express their frustration through passive-aggressive behaviors such as …

- Gossiping
- Withholding information
- Freezing people out
- Doing ONLY what they are told to do
- Consistently arriving late or taking extended breaks
- Finding every loophole possible in policies, procedures, and standards

Staff Stampede

During our first visit to Precise Manufacturing, Scott

conducted one of his favorite reconnaissance missions. He sat in his car at the beginning and end of the day to observe what was happening at the employee entrance. (We've learned you can tell a lot about an organization when you sit in their parking lot.)

At Precise Manufacturing, Scott observed that there's a mad rush for the door at every shift change—and it takes place in a super-condensed 10 minutes. You see, people wait until the last second to arrive. AND it seems like they can't wait to leave.

This vibe plays out inside the building too. About 30 minutes before quitting time, you'll notice that employees begin to stretch out their work. Many start filling in the time by doing non-essential tasks. (You wouldn't want to accidentally be in the middle of something that might prevent you from leaving RIGHT at quitting time, right?) Or our favorite: Somehow it seems to take 25–30 minutes to get packed up and ready to leave. Hmmm. All of that effort by employees to ensure they can walk out the door just as the clock strikes the top of the hour.

Quit and Stay
The last piece of Precise Manufacturing's current culture consists of a quiet-quitting mentality. Precise Manufacturing has historically paid their staff well. They have competitive benefits. The organization has been around for a long time, so people consider them

THINK

to be a reliable and stable employer. And even though employees talk and behave as if they are disgruntled, they are not dissatisfied ENOUGH to risk taking another job. That means Precise Manufacturing's turnover has remained relatively consistent—consistently low. The staff told us that it's easier to put their heads down, do just enough to get by, and ride it out. "I mean—it's only a job—right?"

Ouch!

If that's the overall culture inside of Precise Manufacturing, what did we see happening at each level of the workforce?

HOW PEOPLE ARE BEHAVING
Precise Manufacturing's People

Executive Leaders
At the helm of Precise Manufacturing sits a "team" of very experienced leaders who believe they are smarter than everyone else—including the managers, supervisors, production staff, and customers who are "below" them on the org chart. And that is only their first mistake. With a laser focus on productivity, Precise Manufacturing's executive leaders disseminate their expectations through a very formal process that leaves little room for questions—let alone conversation and thinking.

Middle Managers
Middle managers are groomed to align with executive

THINK

leader decisions. And in their role as "middlemen" they have three primary responsibilities:

1. **Hit your metrics.** Every job has a production goal, and production is king. Hit your metrics, and all is good. Miss your metrics, and you risk your job.
2. **Ensure uniformity.** There is one way to do things, and it is called Standard Work. The organization has invested a lot of resources into developing Standard Work, and leadership sees little to no reason to deviate from the Standard Work that THEY created. Middle managers SHALT NOT DEVIATE.
3. **Positively disperse communications.** Cascading information from the top of the organization to the rest of the company is the third responsibility of middle managers. And they are expected to share the needed information with optimism and total allegiance—no questions asked.

Supervisors

Supervisors are seen as "executers." And they are completely micromanaged. Not only are they given Standard Work procedures for each and every step of the manufacturing process, they are also expected to follow a Standard Work procedure for how they use their time.

Supervisor Time   Standard Work

- 8:00–8:30   Shift transfer
- 8:31–9:00   Production review meeting
- 9:01–11:00   Floor walk
- 11:01–11:45   Computer work
- 11:46–12:30   Lunch break
- 12:31–2:15   Floor walk
- 2:16–3:00   Computer work
- 3:31–4:00   Shift transfer

And by the way, there is Standard Work that outlines exactly how to do a shift transfer, production review meeting, floor walk, etc. No need to think, just follow the Standard Work. Imagine for a minute how you would feel if this was your world. YIKES!

Production Employees
We think you can guess what it feels like to be a production worker at Precise Manufacturing. They are treated just like the cogs in the machinery they work on. Front line employees are considered replaceable.

If you're keeping track, you've probably figured out that working at Precise Manufacturing feels like a soulless, thankless business. From the overall culture to the way employees are treated at each level, it didn't surprise us that the company was seeing some very noticeable drops in productivity and profitability. And in our eyes, the root problem was that employees at every level had stopped actually thinking.

2

We're Too Busy to Think About This $hit

THINK

OK, maybe things are not as bad at your organization as what we found at Precise Manufacturing. But what happens when your executive leaders are **All-Knowing Albertos,** your middle managers are groomed to be **Get Along Garys,** and your staff members end up being **Rodneys, Steves, Evelyns,** and **Julias?** Organizationally—what's the impact of shallow thinking?

You can expect three primary things:

1. Increase in faulty decisions
2. Maintaining the status quo
3. Reduced productivity

Increase in Faulty Decisions

We'll start by looking at how shallow-thinking organizations make inferior decisions. A 2021 Gartner report [1] highlights that poor decision-making costs organizations billions of dollars annually. Frequently, that plays out in how an organization utilizes their resources. When we bring this topic up, some of our clients get a little defensive. They want to talk about how efficient their production lines are, and how they have successfully managed their budgets. Yes, AND ...

Let's expand on the word "resources" and include human capital, time, priorities, and information on our list of organizational resources.

1. **Organizations waste a ton of human capital.** How? They underutilize the skills and abilities of their staff. Like **All-Knowing Alberto,** they ignore the knowledge base that their staff has accumulated. They don't invest in expanding the skills and abilities of their staff—or if they do, they act like **Echo Chamber Evelyn** and ignore their staff input. And they don't delegate—which means the organization is paying supervisory, managerial, and executive wages for work that the

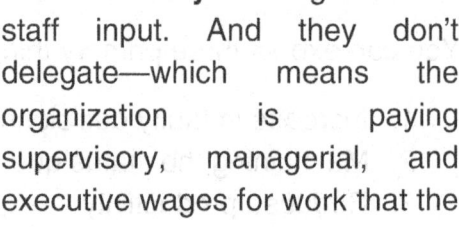

supervisor's, manager's, or executive's STAFF should be doing.

When we first meet an organization's executive team and bring this subject up, we often see skepticism written all over their faces. We get it. We help grow and transform organizations. So, when we suggest that their leaders are not working at their level of responsibility—it sounds extremely self-serving. Yes, AND ...

We're not making this stuff up. In fact, there's a scholarly name for it: "reverse delegation." This concept was first introduced years ago in one of our favorite Harvard Business Review articles, "Management Time: Who's Got the Monkey?" written by William Oncken, Jr., and Donald L. Wass.[2] What exactly is "reverse delegation"? It's when an employee somehow transfers the responsibility for their work back to their manager. Now let's be fair. More often than not, they don't do this overtly. It's subtle, such as when an employee ...

- Presents their manager with a problem without proposing a solution.
- Seeks guidance and approval on tasks they should be able to handle on their own.
- Shares how "overwhelmed" they are.

And leaders, who may believe they are being

helpful or supportive, accept these "monkeys" without thinking (we're looking at you, **Get Along Gary**) and end up doing their employees' jobs.

Combine this with ...

- A misunderstanding of Robert K. Greenleaf's concept of Servant Leadership. [3]
- Some leaders' reluctance to address poor performance.
- The "super-individual contributor trap" where a leader, promoted because of their exceptional performance as an individual contributor, continues to define their value and spend their time on individual tasks.

And you have the perfect storm of wasted human capital. So, the question is ...

Does this sound familiar?

2. **Organizations hemorrhage time.**
Let's just consider meetings. Many studies indicate that the average U.S. supervisor spends 10–12 hours a week in meetings. Honestly, that number seems very low compared to what our clients tell us ... Regardless, the questions we need to be asking include:

THINK

- What's the purpose of the meeting?
- Are those hours well spent?
- Are these meetings productive?
- And who should even attend these meetings?

A great book written by Michael C. Mankins and Eric Garton called Time, Talent, Energy: Overcome Organizational Drag and Unleash Your Team's Productive Power [4] suggests that

- Half of our meetings should not have been scheduled in the first place.
- Fifty percent of the meeting attendees should not have been invited.
- Another chunk of people should have only joined these meetings for a few minutes.

Consider it from this perspective: If anyone is attending a meeting where their insight is unnecessary or duplicative, you are squandering resources.

Let's do some back-of-the-napkin math. If a supervisor, who makes $90,000 a year, spends just five hours a week in unnecessary meetings, that represents about $11,250 a year—wasted. Maybe that doesn't sound too bad to you ... And let's say you have 10 supervisors. That's $112,500 a year.

THINK

Now ask yourself a couple of questions.

- Would you throw away a piece of equipment worth $112k every year?
- Would you pay someone $112k a year to sit at home and do nothing?
- Would you start a fire with $100 bills—1,125 of them?

We certainly hope not. AND when you waste the time of people in your organization—that's exactly what you're doing.

To make all of us just a bit more uncomfortable, remember meetings are not your only organizational time-wasters.

THINK

Consider your organization's

- Inefficient processes.
- Redundancies.
- Procrastination tendencies.
- Propensity to wait for clarification and/or seek permission.
- Interruption habits.
- Rework caused when tasks are delegated before a leader determines what "good" looks like.

Now ask yourself: Are we good stewards of our staff's time? Am I a good steward of MY time?

3. **Organizations pretend to prioritize.**
As strategic planning facilitators, we have sat in countless strategic planning sessions where the board and senior management identify, prioritize, and align around how the organization is going to spend their money and their time. Then, in a matter of days, just like a typical new year's resolution, we see the organization forget its commitment, and we watch them as they move on to other things. It's an all-too-common way that **Terry the Trend Follower** tendencies derail intended priorities.

THINK

Admittedly—there ARE good reasons an organization might change its mind. AND that's not what we're talking about here. Most organizations don't purposefully shift—they drift.

A 2024 Reclaim study says that 98% of workers struggle with setting priorities, [5] and a 2023 Slingshot survey suggests that 25% of U.S. workers actually have no idea what their priorities are. [6]

That means in most organizations, day by day, hour by hour, level by level, independent decisions are being made that don't align with organizational priorities. These decisions are being made because they're expedient, or they're comfortable, or for a dozen other shallow-thinking reasons. And without due diligence, without THINKING, personal preference takes precedence over the organization's agreed-upon priorities.

4. **Organizations bury information.**
Information sharing has been a pain point for organizations since the first entrepreneurs hired their first employees. How do we know? Tammy started her career at Intran, an organization that designed and administered employee attitude surveys. (Since that was 100 years ago, ☺ we now call them Employee Engagement Surveys.) There, she quickly learned that the #1 issue

employees thought they faced was a lack of information. And unfortunately, all these years later, communication still consistently ranks at the top of organizational pain points.

Look at it this way. A report titled "The High Cost of Not Finding Information," published by market research firm IDC [7], suggests that the issue is not a lack of information, but rather that the right people are not connected to the right information at the right time. IDC's latest research finds:

- Employees spend nearly 36% of their time looking for critical information.
- Knowledge workers find the information they need only half of the time.
- 61% of knowledge workers must access four or more systems to do their jobs, while another 13% have to look at 11 or more systems before they can get the information they need. [8]

When employees can't access the information they need, it's a sign that resources aren't being used wisely—which results in poor decision-making within organizations.

Maintaining the Status Quo
We wrote a book in 2021 about "shattering the status quo" because most organizations don't consciously choose to hit the repeat button and stagnate. More

often than not, they simply make first one and then another decision to play it safe. But just ask any professional athlete, playing it safe only gives your opponents the opportunity catch up. That's why maintaining the organization's status quo is the second consequence of shallow thinking.

So, what happens when companies embrace the status quo?

1. **Giants fall.**

In 1998 Nokia (which had been in business since 1865) became the world's largest mobile phone manufacturer, running right past Motorola, when they manufactured and sold their 100,000,000th mobile phone. And by the end of 2007 they owned **49.4%** of the mobile phone market. That's domination!

But things were brewing behind the scenes. Apple released its first iPhone in June of 2007 and Google released their smart phone operating system, Andriod, in September of 2008. And what happened next is the subject of myriad academic research papers. [9] [10]

Nokia ignored these new technologies. By 2011 their market share had dropped to 14% and a CNNIC survey found that 53% of current Nokia customers were planning to switch to a smart phone when their contracts renewed.

On September 3, 2013, Nokia sold the company's mobile phone business to Microsoft. Oh, how quickly the mighty can fall when they decide to play it safe.

2. **Opportunities are missed.**
The merger of America Online (AOL) and Time Warner in 2001 was touted as a landmark moment. It was a fusion of old media and new, poised to dominate the burgeoning digital landscape. The vision was grand. The mashup of Time Warner's content empire (magazines, movies, cable TV) with AOL's massive online subscriber base should have created an internet powerhouse. Instead, this case study of missed opportunities ultimately paved the way for the rise of giants like Google and Facebook.[11]

Missed opportunity one: AOL/Time Warner clung to its dial-up subscriber model and failed to anticipate the rapid growth of broadband internet. Their sluggish response allowed competitors to attract and keep customers that appreciated quicker response times and richer online experiences.

Missed opportunity two: Internal infighting plagued the new company. Instead of leveraging these differences of opinion into opportunities for growth and innovation, AOL/Time Warner became a battleground of competing interests.

Missed opportunity three: While AOL/Time Warner was grappling with internal issues, companies like Google and Facebook were rapidly innovating and building their own digital empires. Google found its place in the market by developing a superior search engine and advertising platform. And Facebook, focused on social networking, revolutionized how people connected and shared information online.

Isn't it interesting what happens when you waste time on the wrong things?

3. **Someone else ends up eating your lunch.**
   Few stories are as cautionary as Blockbuster's blunder. [12][13][14] Blockbuster Video, once the undisputed king of home video rentals, famously had the chance to acquire a fledgling organization called Netflix. This decision, or rather the lack thereof, has become a textbook example of short-sightedness and a monumental missed opportunity that reshaped the entertainment landscape.

   The year was 2000. Netflix, then a mail-order DVD rental service, was struggling to gain traction. They approached Blockbuster, the behemoth with thousands of brick-and-mortar stores, with an acquisition offer for a mere $50 million. Blockbuster, riding high on its dominant market share and flush with cash, actually scoffed at the offer. They viewed Netflix as a niche player and a minor annoyance rather than a serious threat.

This dismissal would prove to be a catastrophic miscalculation. Blockbuster's leadership, blinded by their current success and stuck in the status quo, continued to focus on their familiar and profitable brick-and-mortar stores and completely missed the up-and-coming age of streaming.

The consequences of Blockbuster's short-sightedness were devastating. As Netflix's popularity soared, Blockbuster's revenue plummeted. Their once-crowded stores became ghost towns, symbols of a bygone era. In 2010, Blockbuster filed for bankruptcy, a dramatic fall from grace for a company that had been a cultural icon less than a decade earlier.

Meanwhile, Netflix went on to become a global streaming giant, with millions of subscribers worldwide. As of 2025, they are still a dominant force in the entertainment industry, producing original content and shaping the way people consume movies, television, and more.

Maybe **we** should listen instead of laughing when someone asks us to consider something new and different.

Reduced Productivity

Organizations that don't teach and/or encourage deep thinking experience a third consequence: a reduction in productivity. So, how does shallow thinking mess with efficiency? Let's break it down.

1. **Processes suck.**
   Organizations that don't emphasize thinking typically have inefficient processes. Some organizations cling to outdated methodologies. (Like **Echo Chamber Evelyn,** they rely too much on their current point of view.)

   On the other end of the continuum, some companies implement new processes without fully understanding the impact of their decisions. (Sounds like **Running Rodney,** right?) We've seen both. And in either case, the research tells us that this lack of systems thinking leads to organizational redundancies, unnecessary steps, and bottlenecks—all of which slow down

operations, waste valuable time, and irritate the heck out of people.

What kind of productivity impact are we actually talking about? The research varies by industry. But if this is happening in your organization you might be experiencing a productivity dip between 10 and 50%. Ouch!

2. **Iteration and continuous improvement are nonexistent.**
It's one thing to not get it done right the first time. It's a much bigger deal when organizations don't learn through iteration and don't grow by embracing a continuous improvement mentality.

We know. A lot of people think iteration and continuous improvement are just trendy buzzwords. And they're wrong. Iteration and continuous improvement can have a major impact on a company's bottom line. Here's the research that backs up that statement.

Faster time to market: A study by the Product Development and Management Association (PDMA) [15] found that companies using iterative prototyping reported a 43% decrease in time-to-market compared to traditional methods.

Reduced costs and waste: There are hundreds of studies on Lean manufacturing and Six Sigma methodologies that consistently demonstrate the savings associated with continuous improvement. To use our own organization as a tiny example of the potential of continuous improvement initiatives, the related projects that BecomeMore Group facilitated in 2024 saved our customers more than $5 million. And we're a consulting firm with just five full-time staff!

Increased innovation and revenue: Iteration fuels innovation by allowing companies and the people who work there the opportunity to experiment, to learn from failures, and to quickly adapt. This can lead to the development of new products, services, and solutions that generate additional revenue. A study published in the Journal of Product Innovation Management [16] found that companies using iterative design methodologies reported a 75% higher success rate.

3. **People don't like working there.**
One of the things that drives us just a little bit crazy is how people talk about employee engagement. Let's face it—the concept of employee engagement isn't tough. And we don't need a bunch of fancy words to describe it. It's really about whether or not people enjoy working for your organization.

If they enjoy the work they're doing, if they like their boss, if they feel like they're making a difference, and if they get along with their co-workers—they will go the extra mile. If ANY of those four things are missing ... most of the time your employees are probably trying to look busy while they wait for the 5 o'clock whistle that signals the end of the workday. If this is what's happening in your organization, your numbers probably look something like this:

- Productivity has been dropping (most organizations see an 8—20% annual decline).
- Absenteeism increases (the average increase is about 37%).
- And while it's a bit tough to isolate the data, research strongly suggests that disengaged employees are more likely to make mistakes and/or produce lower quality work.

What's the Impact of Shallow Thinking?
It ain't good.

We see this all the time when we're invited to meet with new clients. Organizations underestimate—even cultivate—the negative effects of shallow thinking. They take shortcuts in their decision-making processes, they accept mediocracy, they overlook inefficiencies, and they blame reduced performance

THINK

on the wrong things, which ultimately leads to a weaker bottom line.

Now let's take a look at what can happen when individuals—and whole organizations—invest in deeper thinking.

3

The Power of Thinking

THINK

Looking at the Precise Manufacturing, Nokias and Blockbusters of the world illustrates the pitfalls of organizations that don't think. Accepting the status quo and pressing the easy button has real, lasting, and negative impacts on success. So, what happens when an organization invests in thinking more deeply?

Let us introduce you to Ascend.

At this small professional services firm where Amelia (the CEO), recognized an organizational pattern. Her team was technically proficient. Most of their projects were considered successful. And their clients were satisfied. All of which was fine.

And that was the problem. Things were fine, not excellent. They were good. Amelia wanted Ascend to be exceptional.

What Was Happening?

The team had fallen into a rut. They would talk with clients, hear a concern, and then bring a "tried and true" solution to the table. You know that saying, "Everything looks like a nail when you have a hammer"? That's what Ascend was doing: over-applying a small set of "safe" solutions. And while "safe" was steady, Ascend's ...

- Bottom line had straight-lined.
- Employees were beginning to act "bored-out."
- Clients started seeing issues resurface, after applying Ascend's solutions.
- Competitors were slowly gaining market share.

During one of our executive coaching sessions, Amelia had an aha moment. She realized that the organization was "reacting" instead of "thinking." Clients would often use the same words to describe their organizational issues. And when the staff heard those words—they would stop digging and start running.

Amelia had an organization full of **Running Rodneys.**

In her push to be productive and efficient she had encouraged the staff to push the easy button instead of digging deep, asking questions, and truly thinking things through. The staff's habit had become: See the problem, kill the problem. Amelia realized that this shallow thinking was not going to propel the organization forward or enable them to reach their long-term goals.

The Result?
We worked with Amelia for three years. We helped her and her teams see where they were short-cutting their own thinking.

In the following chapters, we'll share many of the tactics they used to deepen their thinking and create the future they desired. And then, we'll tell you the rest of Amelia's story.

4
The Mind Games We Play

THINK

Let's be real, we all like to think our brains are these amazing, super-efficient machines that process information flawlessly. And here's the thing: Your brain is more like a quirky, slightly unreliable teammate than a supercomputer. Our brains have their own agendas, their own weird habits, and sometimes, well, our brains simply mess up.

Why? Neuroscience has a lot to say about it. Truly, our brains are amazing—AND they're flawed. And those flaws ... ? They're actually baked right into the way our brains work.

Brain Shortcuts: The Bias Bonanza

Imagine you're walking down a dark alley and you hear a strange noise. In that moment, your brain doesn't take the time to do a full risk assessment. Instead, in an instant your brain starts screaming "Danger Will Robinson, DANGER!" (If you're a child of the '60s or '70s, you'll get this reference. If not, you'll want to check out the "Lost in Space" TV show.)

So why do our brains immediately jump to the conclusion that we're in danger? It's really about survival. All of us are born with a brain hack that allows us to make quick decisions. Cognitive psychologists, who study how people think, learn, and process information, sometimes call these cognitive biases—and there are a bunch of them.

Confirmation Bias: Remember **Echo Chamber Evelyn**? She suffers from confirmation bias. Regardless of ALL the information that is available, people who have confirmation bias favor information that <u>confirms</u> their existing beliefs and experiences and <u>ignores</u> contrary evidence.

For instance, let's say your favorite sports team is the Kansas City Chiefs. You've watched them for years. And the 2024–25 season is special. They've won the last two Super Bowls. They have some amazingly good players. Patrick Mahomes, Travis Kelce, George Karlaftis, and Chris Jones to name a few. And they

THINK

are headed into the 2025 Super Bowl with a 17 and 2 record. You know that they are going to win. Why? Because they are the BEST team. Not just this year—but basically every year since Mahomes took over as quarterback. And they know how to win big games. Been there. Done that. Of course, they are going to win.

Except ...

Your confirmation bias may have overlooked a couple of important facts.

- The Chiefs played 11 games this season that were decided by 1 point or less.
- They did not score more than 30 points in a single game over the course of the entire 2024 season.
- When the Chiefs bested the Eagles the previous year, it took a heroic effort including three unanswered touchdowns in the second half—and a game-winning field goal in the final seconds.

If you follow American football, you know the outcome of this story. The Chiefs lost their 2025 Super Bowl opportunity—badly. If you look at a wider perspective of the data, you'd find that the Chiefs actually repeated a pattern that many fans with confirmation bias overlooked: tight games with a low-scoring offense. And (unfortunately for Tammy) this time the

Chiefs didn't have the juice to pull the game out in the second half.

Availability Bias: Early 2025 saw some really high-profile plane crashes. On January 29 an American Airlines regional jet collided with a U.S. Army Black Hawk helicopter, killing 67 people. Two days later, on January 31, a medical jet crashed in Philadelphia, killing a young girl, her mother, and four crew members.

In January and February 2025 there were 119 aviation accidents, according to the National Transportation Safety Board.[17] Sixteen of those accidents were fatal.

If these examples lead you to believe that flying is really dangerous, you may be **Terry the Trend Follower** who has availability bias. Availability bias happens when your brain recalls recent and/or easily available data instead of looking for accurate and/or thorough data.

So just how dangerous is flying? In the United States in 2022 there were 44,546 transportation deaths. Of those deaths …

- 42,514 involved highway motor vehicles (cars and trucks).
- 983 were railway accidents.

- 686 were boating and commercial watercraft accidents.
- 357 involved on-demand commuter aircraft, air taxis, and general aviation.
- 5 deaths involved large commercial airlines.

Considering that U.S. air traffic navigators [18] coordinate travel for over 45,000 flights and 2.9 million airline flyers <u>every day</u>—your chances of death-via-air-travel are extremely low. Don't let availability bias push you to think otherwise.

Anchoring Bias: Imagine you're shopping for a used car and the first car you look at is a sleek sports car with a sticker price of $30,000. Even though you know you want something much more practical, that $30,000 figure becomes an "anchor" in your mind. Your brain has latched onto the idea that fancy sports cars cost $30,000. Then, as you continue your research you find a low-milage, practical sedan that costs $22,000. And bam! You decide that the sedan is a great deal.

Why? Because you just might be **Sound Bite Stev e** and you have formed an anchor to the initial, higher-price vehicle. Which makes the sedan appear like a better deal in comparison—EVEN though the actual market value of the sedan is closer to $20,000.

Conformity Bias: Ever been in a group text where everyone's like, "Burgers tonight!" while secretly you're dreaming of sushi, but you don't speak up? Yeah, that's conformity bias whispering in your ear. Or you're in a meeting, and someone suggests something totally off-base, and you're thinking, "Nope, that's a terrible idea," and you ... don't say anything? Or how about when someone tells a joke that makes no sense, at least to you, and you force out a laugh because everyone else is chuckling?

We've all been there, done that. It's that feeling of wanting to just blend in, to not be the weird one. To just say yes. And hey, sometimes it's no big deal, right? It makes things easy. It keeps the peace. And you don't end up looking stupid or appearing disagreeable.

Yes, AND ... If everyone's just going along with the flow, who's going to bring up the good ideas? Who's going to say, "Wait a minute, maybe we should try this instead?" That's where **Get Along Gary** gets us into trouble. By not asking questions or challenging the logic, we end up not fully understanding. Or we lose out on gathering different perspectives. Or we just end up doing the same things over and over again because **everyone** is falling into the conformity bias trap and is, well, just trying to get along.

Lake Wobegon Bias: Garrison Keillor, creator and host of A Prairie Home Companion [19], described Lake Wobegon as "a place where all the women are strong, all the men are good-looking, and all the children are above average." And while this is a humorous way of describing this bias, being an **All-Knowing Alberto** is not cool. It means you lack self-awareness. It means you overestimate your own knowledge and abilities. And there's a good chance that it means you are being arrogant.

Most of us don't intend to be arrogant—so it's not easy for us to recognize when we're being **All-Knowing Albertos**. Maybe this story will help:

A few years back, Tammy needed to have her knees replaced. So, she researched the procedure and began collecting recommendations for orthopedic surgeons. Once she settled on a surgeon and figured out her work schedule, Tammy met with the surgeon and explained what she wanted to do: replace both knees during a single surgery in early October. That would provide 12 weeks of recovery and physical therapy time before she had to go back to work after the first of the year.

The surgeon listened politely and after Tammy laid out her grand plan, he asked one very simple and direct question: "Are you the surgeon, or am I?" Yep,

Tammy was being an **All-Knowing Alberto.**

Arbitrary Inference Bias, which we call **Jumping to Conclusions:** You've sent a text to a friend, inviting them to dinner. Historically, they respond right away. And after five minutes you still haven't heard from them and your mind is racing.

- ✓ Why are they ignoring me?
- ✓ What did I say or do that ticked them off?

After 20 minutes, you're obsessing.

- ✓ They have completely blown me off.
- ✓ They don't want to be my friend anymore!

This is a perfect example of **Jumping Julia**. She is inserting a negative interpretation into the situation without sufficient and/or corresponding evidence. In other words, she's identifying and believing her imagined, worst-case scenario.

Arbitrary Inference Bias typically takes two main forms. "Mind reading," where we assume we know what others are thinking. And "fortune telling," where we predict negative outcomes. Both involve making leaps of logic without a lick of factual evidence.

Action Bias: Scott is a huge soccer fan. So, when

THINK

we found some research around soccer and action bias—we just HAD to share it. Here's the skinny ...

Researchers Michael Bar-Eli, Ofer H. Azar, Ilana Ritov, Yael Keidar-Levin, and Galit Schein decided to review soccer penalty kicks and document where the ball was kicked, where the goalkeeper jumped, and whether or not a goal was scored. [20] They discovered something interesting. Goalkeepers that jumped left or right after the kick saved 20% of the goals. Goalies, however, that stayed in the middle and didn't jump at all blocked 33% of the kicks. That's a huge competitive advantage.

Now—this data is not in any way proprietary. And you would expect that once goalkeepers understood the data, they would make the decision to stay smack dab in the middle to increase their odds of blocking the kick. But no. Only 6% of goalies stay put. The rest fall prey to Action Bias and dive either left or right. They are **Running Rodneys**. They believe that doing something—ANYTHING—is better than doing nothing at all.

And before we get all judgy about their choices—let's look at ourselves.

Have you ever been stuck in traffic, gotten off the highway, and taken an alternative route? All without consulting Google Maps? That's action bias. Sitting there, barely making any progress at all, was probably driving you nuts. And while you had no idea if getting off the highway was going to save you time—MOVING made you feel like you were doing something productive. MOVING made you feel as if you were in control. MOVING made you feel better. Nice to meet you, **Running Rodney**. ☺

These biases aren't just quirks; they're hardwired into our brains. Research shows they influence everything from our financial decisions to our political views. They're leftover survival mechanisms that have gone a bit haywire in our modern world. AND we don't have to succumb to these mind games. We can actually reboot our brains to ensure that we're THINKING, not reacting. Let's talk about how.

Part 2
The ROADD to Deeper Thinking

5
Getting on the ROADD

THINK

Alright. We understand that our brains are hardwired to be reactive. We get that we all have cognitive biases. We know that we live in a world that rewards instant responses, quick turnarounds, and witty banter.

And ... What if we slowed down? No, not a full stop. Just a pause. What if we purposefully and intentionally took a moment to THINK?

A 2012 study by Heather A. Butler [21] suggests that adults who engage in a structured process of thinking have better outcomes. And that is where the **ROADD™** model comes in. **ROADD** is a thinking process that expands perspectives, levels up learning, and enables us to deepen our thinking.

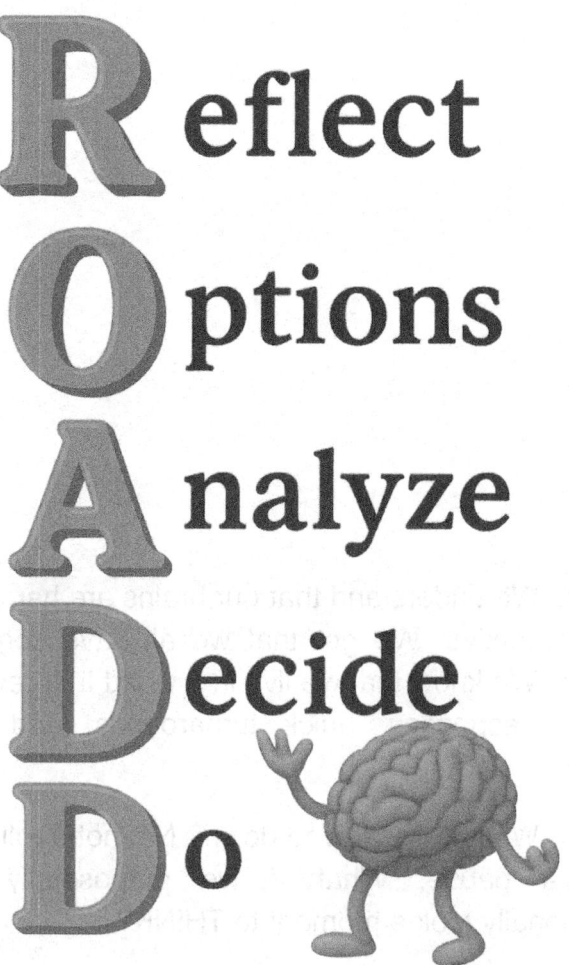

Reflect
Options
Analyze
Decide
Do

THINK

Simply put, **ROADD** is a "roaddmap" that can help us overcome our surface-level thinking, our built-in brain "roadblocks," and cognitive bias. ☺

Let's take a drive down the **ROADD** together.

R = Reflect

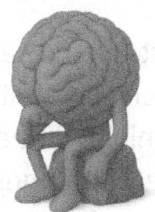

Reflect is the art of digging into what's already in our brains. It's about cataloging what you think you know, identifying the assumptions and/or logic leaps you're making, and spotting the biases that just might be messing with your head.

Think of it like cleaning out your mental attic. When you head up to the attic you just might find some hidden treasure. AND, you'll also find some cobwebs that need to be cleaned up and a bunch of musty junk that probably needs to be tossed.

Research tells us that reflection allows learners (yes, that means you) to make sense of their experiences, connect them to other experiences, and apply this learning to future situations. [22]

Reflection also helps people examine and improve thinking. Technically, this is called metacognition and it's the awareness and understanding of your own thought processes. [23] [24]

While working with clients, Tammy and Scott often

THINK

refer to Tasha Eurick's research.[25] on self-awareness. She suggests that 95% of us believe we are self-aware—when less than 15% of us are actually self-aware. So where do you fall? Are you self-aware or not? One way to think about self-awareness is to ask yourself if you know how you think.

Do you know your COGNATIVE strengths and weaknesses? Can you discern between things that are easy for you to think through and things that are difficult for you to think through? Do you recognize when you make logic leaps or fill in information gaps? And do you have the awareness to change your thinking strategy when something you are doing isn't working for you? Understanding these things about yourself comes from a fair amount of reflection.

If you are saying "no" and "never" to these questions … you might have cognitive bias. (#JeffFoxworthy)

You might think about this first step in **ROADD** as the process of setting a baseline. Reflecting helps you clarify:

- What are you trying to accomplish?
- What does success look like?
- What do you know about the subject?
- How does this align with your prior experiences?

- What are your beliefs (assumptions, logic leaps, biases) around the subject?
- What could you do to help you think things through more clearly?

O = Options

Many of our cognitive biases encourage us to find ONE right answer. Couple that with our formal schooling, where our textbooks provided us with one perspective and our tests rewarded us when we checked the "right" box—and you can understand how we've been programmed to see the problem, kill the problem. Tammy refers to this as "Michael's [her husband's] Search for Black Pants", which goes something like this.

Michael: I need black pants ...

20 seconds later ...

Michael: I just ordered a pair on Amazon. 36x38 inches. 5-star rating. $30 bucks. They're going to be delivered this afternoon.

Yes, that's expedient. AND ... black pants may not just be black pants. Different pants will fit, feel, and look different once they're on. You may need black pants for a variety of occasions like work, a formal event, or even gardening in the backyard. And heck—if Michael had just taken a moment longer, he may have discovered that he already had a pair of perfect black pants in his closet—tucked way back in the corner. But Michael didn't pause to consider options and alternatives. He just killed the problem and checked it off his to-do list. Sound familiar?

Honestly, many of us think this way most of the time. AND ... there are some really great gifts in considering our options instead.

Have you ever been part of an amazing brainstorming session? You know what we're talking about. That time when the team really got into it and the juices were flowing. Sure, in the beginning the team threw out some really obvious and typical solutions. Then— all of a sudden—things started clicking and some potentially powerful ideas came to the forefront. That's divergent thinking at work. [26] Divergent thinking research emphasizes that unique and creative solutions emerge only AFTER the most conventional and obvious ideas are brought to the table.

What else? Why should we take the time to identify options and alternatives? The research tells us that when we deliberately identify options and alternatives we ...

- Develop additional expertise. [27]
- Increase mental agility—which translates into increased resourcefulness and resiliency. [28]

THINK

- Improve strategic decision-making. [29]
- Feel more empowered—which reduces stress and improves well-being. [30]

This should be enough motivation for us to take this second step down the **ROADD** and look for a third, fourth, or even a fifth option.

A = Analyze

Analyze, the third step in **ROADD**, is where you put on your mental detective hat. It's about digging into the details, breaking down complex information, identifying patterns, and evaluating evidence.

At BecomeMore Group a day doesn't go by where we don't use a very simple analysis tool that we call The Growth Questions™. After every sales call, workshop, and even our internal meetings we ask ourselves three important questions.

- What worked?
- What didn't work?
- What will we do differently next time?

This simple habit is the reason our team is excelling. It's why 95% of our clients are repeat customers. And it's why we've been able to improve our bottom line. It's been our "not-so-secret" sauce for over 30 years.

We know analysis works. And the research supports our point of view.

1. **Analysis improves outcomes:** Let's look at things that all of us do, like eating and spending money. A book by Richard Thaler and Cass Sunstein called Nudge [31] makes the case that consistently tracking and analyzing expenditures leads to increased savings and reduced debt. And it's the same with weight loss. A meta-analysis published in the Journal of the Academy of Nutrition and Dietetics [32] found that self-monitoring—particularly food journaling AND the accompanying analysis—helps people lose more weight.

   How does that translate? This research suggests that when we dive into the details and look at trends and themes, it provides us with information that can help us make better decisions—and ultimately have improved outcomes. Thomas Davenport wrote the primer on this topic, Competing on the Analytics: The New Science of Winning. [33] And if you want to be entertained while you're being convinced, you can always watch the movie MoneyBall starring Brad Pitt.

2. **Analysis helps us overcome brain biases:** Daniel Kahneman's book called "Thinking, Fast and Slow," [34] makes the case that

confirmation and availability biases distort our judgement. However, when we analyze options and alternatives—and the data that comes with it—we give ourselves the chance to step away from our kneejerk, preconceived notions and confront our biases head on. And that leads to better-informed decisions.

3. **Analysis allows us to verify our sources:** "Fake news" was not a phrase we heard growing up. In fact, in the '60s and '70s U.S. news anchors were some of the most trusted people in the country. That's not true today. According to myriad recent surveys, the news media is considered one of the LEAST trusted institutions in this country right now. The institution that typically sits at the bottom of these surveys? Congress.

We bring that up, not to get into a political conversation, but to point out that where we get our information matters. One of our favorite papers published on this topic is titled "Lazy, Not Biased: Susceptibility to Partisan Fake News."[35] And like the title suggests—we probably aren't stupid. We might be biased. There is, however, a very good chance that we're lazy!

That means one of the most critical things we can do during analysis is evaluate our sources.

THINK

We need to:

- **Consider the author(s).** Who created the information? Are they experts in the field? What are their credentials? Is the organization reputable? Do they have a track record of accuracy?
- **Look at the evidence.** Is the information supported by evidence, such as data, research, or expert opinions? Are the sources of evidence clearly cited?
- **Think about THEIR why.** Why was the information created? Is it to inform, persuade, or entertain? Is there a potential conflict of interest? Does the source present a balanced perspective, or is it heavily one-sided?
- **Seek out cross-references.** Don't rely on a single source. Compare information from multiple credible sources to get a more complete picture. And look for consistency and agreement among different sources.
- **Check for accuracy.** Is the information factually correct? Are there any errors or inconsistencies? And what do fact-checker websites like Snopes, FactCheck.org, and PolitiFact have to say? These resources often provide detailed analyses of claims and identify misinformation.

Evaluating our sources is absolutely crucial in today's information-saturated world. It's the difference between making informed decisions and being misled.

4. **Analysis reduces risk:** Finally, let's talk about risk and rewards. It would be great if our world worked in a "it's either right or wrong" fashion. Unfortunately, that's not the case. Many of life's choices come with BOTH good and bad consequences.

Consider a healthcare organization that is operating in the red. They need to break even to stay in business. They have less than 15 days of operating cash. And they've been running in the red for the last 24 months. Do they continue to offer a line of service that is costing them more money than it brings in? Or do they cut that service to ensure the organization's sustainability? OK—let's make it a little more difficult to decide. IF they made the decision to cut that service it would mean that 500 patients would have nowhere else to go. And their health would surely deteriorate.

This situation, like soooo many others, reflects the choices that many of us face. There is no perfect solution. And there may not even be a solution we're truly happy with. Why? Because we don't like the consequences and/or the downside of any of our options.

All of us have faced this kind of situation in our lives. And it can be paralyzing. That's where analysis can help. We've learned from game theory [36] and behavioral economics [37] that when we evaluate options, we can see potential pitfalls before we encounter them. And then, we can utilize that information to think through how different choices interact, what outcomes might result, and what risks and rewards we're willing to take.

If you're a gamer, this makes complete sense to you. Your choice might not result in a PERFECT outcome. But you live to play another day.

Research tells us you can achieve these same kinds of results when you analyze options and alternatives in the real world. The analysis can help you think through these very difficult choices and identify a solution that enables you to achieve your goal while you mitigate the downside as much as possible. [38] [39]

5. **Analysis deepens our understanding:** A really cool thing happens when we spend time in analysis. Our brains start making all sorts of connections. Ever hear of Bloom's Taxonomy? [40] It's a framework that looks at

different levels of learning and explains the objective of thinking at each level.

We've modified it a bit. Bloom's original includes six levels, where the bottom three are analysis, synthesis, and evaluation. We believe that Bloom's analysis level is the gateway to deeper levels of learning that include both synthesis and evaluation. So we use a taxonomy with four levels to explain the role of analysis.

BecomeMore Taxonomy

Level 1: Knowledge	You can recall and/or repeat back something that you have learned.
Level 2: Comprehension	You can explain what you know in your own words.
Level 3: Application	You can take what you know and apply it to new and different situations and circumstances.
Level 4: Analysis	You can look at what you know and can differentiate, compare, contrast, connect, question, and judge.

When we are in analysis, our brains start differentiating, comparing and contrasting, connecting ideas to another, and actually questioning and judging our information, assumptions, sources, and data. This happens because of the TOOLS we use in analysis.

Analysis is powerful. As Colin Powell once said, "Good and solid analysis and a formal way of looking at a problem [are the core ingredients of good decisions]."

D = Decide

After all that reflecting, option-exploring, and analyzing, it's time to pull the trigger and decide. But hold on, it's not just about flipping a coin and hoping for the best. This step in the **ROADD** model is about taking ownership, making a conscious choice, and mapping out the path forward. It's where we move from the realm of "what ifs" to the domain of "what now?"

Think of it like this ... You've been planning your next vacation.

Reflect: You've reflected on the number of vacation days you have left, the timeframe you have available, and the money you have in your travel fund.

Options: You've looked at what you thought was possible, considering all those constraints. You did a bit of online research and even asked AI for recommendations. Then you took a few friends out for drinks and asked them what they might recommend.

Analyze: Afterwards you compared and contrasted your options based on weather, travel time, activities, and what you know your travel partner would prefer.

Now you've got to make a choice.

Decide is about making the choice AND owning the choice. It's the transition from contemplation to action. And it's at this point in the journey when we face the reality that:

- A choice needs to be made.
- Not taking action and/or delaying making a decision is still a choice.
- WE are responsible for the outcomes of our choice.

For some of us, that's scary. If that's you, consider that could be the <u>old</u> you. Why? Because if you follow the **ROADD**, you will be making the best decision you can in the time frame you have and with the information that is available to you.

Will it be a perfect decision? No. Very few decisions are perfect.

Will it work? Will it solve the problem? Will it move you and your team/organization/family further down the road toward the goals and objectives you want to achieve? Yes. Again, why? Because you have engaged in deeper thinking. And deeper thinking results in improved decision-making.[41]

Remember when we talked about how analysis reduces risk? The truth is that no matter what decision is made, there will be consequences. Some of those consequences will be good. And even really good decisions often come with both good and not-so-good consequences. That's the reality of many of the circumstances we find ourselves in. If we've followed the **ROADD** we should know that we made a good choice. And we need to have the courage to embrace and live with the consequences of the decision we made.

D = Do

Do is this wonderful blend of conviction and pragmatism. It's the implementation of decisions. It's how you make your decision a reality. For example, if you were to decide without doing it would be like choosing where you want to go on vacation and never actually taking that vacation.

Here is what's really interesting about that. Peter Gollwitzer's research [42] tells us that when people determine WHAT they are going to DO they are more likely to actually follow through on their decision. And this isn't just theory; it's extremely practical.

THINK

Imagine you've analyzed your spending habits and found that you're spending more money than you're earning. You also realized that you're spending a big chunk of your budget on eating out. Deciding is making the decision that you are going to spend less money each month eating out. Doing looks like setting a reduced budget for eating out, creating a weekly meal plan, determining what day of the week you will go grocery shopping, and unsubscribing from food delivery apps. Doing translates decisions into concrete actions.

Reflect
Options
Analyze
Decide
Do

Doing also comes with a huge gift. When we feel a sense of control over our actions and believe we've developed a plan that will help us succeed, we are not only more committed—we are also more confident. And that confidence will help us persevere when and if challenges arise.[43]

The double Ds of **Decide** and **Do** are not about impulsive action; they're about deliberate and informed action. They're about moving from a state of analysis to a state of purposeful execution. And they're when we take control of our outcomes. [44]

The ROADD to Deeper Thinking

The **ROADD** model is more than just a set of steps; it's a mindset. It's about cultivating a lifelong habit of curiosity, critical thinking, and open-mindedness. It's about embracing the complexity of the world and finding meaning in the midst of it all. It's about leveling up, and yes, Becoming More. So, the next time you face an important issue, begin your journey with a little drive down the **ROADD** to deeper thinking.

Part 3
Cultivating a Culture of Thinking

We've already made the case for creating an organizational culture of deep thinking. So now the question is: How? How do you encourage, support, and cultivate deep thinking at an organizational level? Here's the good news.

1. It can be done!
2. It doesn't take a ton of money!!
3. You don't have to overhaul your current culture to incorporate deeper thinking!!!
4. It doesn't require a huge new corporate initiative!!!!

You just need to try on a few organizational thinking

tactics and see what sticks.

So, what are organizational thinking tactics? They are a series of small shifts in organizational behavior. And when you commit to a few of these behavior shifts you can experience some pretty big benefits. [45] [46] [47]

If you've read our book Chief Optimization Officer, you know that we believe in incremental growth (if you haven't, what are you waiting for!?! ☺). Yes, people are drawn to BIG wins. No doubt, BIG changes make headlines and are the basis for great stories. AND ... small, incremental growth wins in the long run.

People often apply this concept to product launches and/or process improvement. With a little deep thinking however, it can also be applied to internal organizational growth and maturity. In other words, don't bring out the banners and ballons to announce that you're going to create a culture of deep organizational thinking next year. Instead, if you want to create a culture of organizational thinking, make some <u>subtle</u> <u>shifts</u> in the way you do things.

We introduce a model in our Elevate Your Leadership™ workshop called the Leadership Ladder™. The Leadership Ladder model provides leaders with a framework to coach, grow, and hold staff accountable.

There are four rungs on the ladder. And as with all ladders, you start at the bottom.

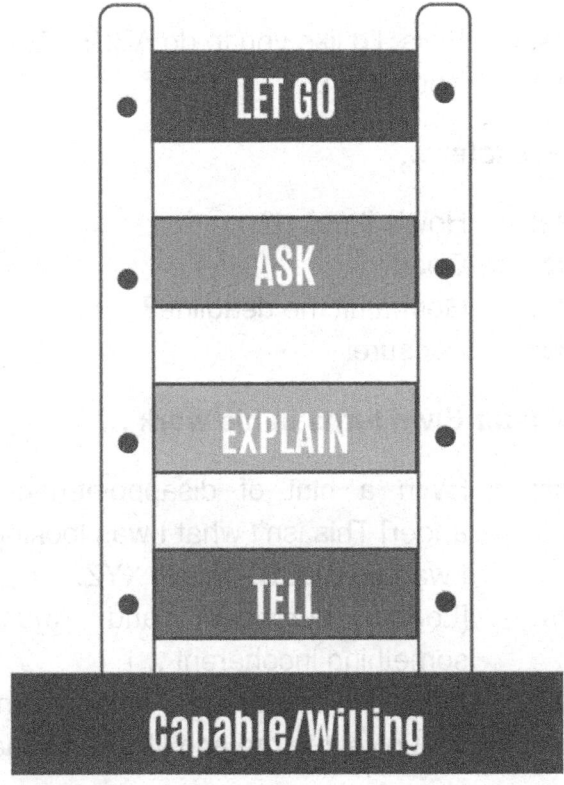

LEADERSHIP LADDER™

Without fail, when we talk through the model in class, someone will say something like, "We don't have time for rungs 2 and 3. We've got deadlines and work that HAS to be done."

Yes, AND ...

THINK

If we don't TAKE the time to Explain and Ask, we end up doing something we call bipolar leadership. Bipolar leadership happens when a leader jumps from rung 1 (Tell) to rung 4 (Let Go). And it goes something like this:

Boss: Elvis, I'd like you to do ABCD. Got it?
Elvis: Yep. ABCD.

Two days later ...

Boss: How's it going?
Elvis: Good.
Boss: Gonna hit the deadline?
Elvis: For sure!

A week later Elvis turns in his work ...

Boss: [With a hint of disappointment and anger] This isn't what I was looking for. I wanted ABCD. This is XYZ.
Elvis: [Looks surprised and mumbles something incoherent ...]
Boss: Well—the meeting is this afternoon. Just give it to me and I'll get it done.

Sound familiar?

We see this all the time in organizations. And if you don't take a moment to walk down the **ROADD**, you might miss the fact that Elvis actually did what he thought his boss wanted him to do. He got the

THINK

information and took action (notice the **Running Rodney** behavior).

Elvis, however, was set up to fail when his boss Informed him and then jumped directly to Let Go. The boss then made it worse when he didn't take the time again on round 2 to Explain and Ask. Instead, the boss took the work back and informed Elvis that HE would get it done in time for the afternoon meeting. (Don't miss the shades of **Sound Bite Steve** and **All-Knowing Alberto** in the boss's behavior.)

In this example, Elvis' thinking (and work) was diminished. And it taught Elvis that his boss has all the "right" answers. That means Elvis doesn't need to think—he just needs to DO. Oh, and be able to read his boss's mind. ☺

Ouch!

How does this apply to organizational thinking tactics? Organizational thinking tactics actually support leaders in rungs 2 and 3. They are simple behavior changes that don't take a tremendous amount of time—yet still make a big difference. And when companies systematically incorporate them into their daily work habits, they find that their LEADERS are quietly and subtly shifting the organization's thinking culture—even as they tap into the brilliance and thinking skills of each member on their team.

THINK

One Size Does Not Fit All

In the next few chapters, we're going to introduce you to a collection of our tried-and-true organizational thinking tactics.

1. The Growth Questions
2. Stay Stupid Longer™ (SSL)
3. Readers are Thinkers
4. Carve out Thinking Time
5. Expand Facilitation & Problem Solving
6. Lead Them Down the **ROADD**

AND, we don't want you to swallow them hook, line, and sinker. (We're not trying to make you into **Jumping Julias**, after all.) The organizational thinking tactics we're sharing with you are options— not a full-fledged blueprint. Simply ...

- Read them.
- Find one that you believe will give your organization the biggest bang for the buck.
- Try it on for size.
- See what happens.
- Iterate to make it yours.

Once your leaders have that organizational thinking tactic under their belts, choose the next one. Add it to your organization's tool kit. See what happens. Play with it until you see improved results. Then make your next choice.

Some of these organizational thinking tactics will work for you. Others will not. What we DO know is that as you add and embed these new habits, you will see and experience improved organizational results. And do yourself a favor ... benchmark before you start. Ask yourself:

- Where are decisions being made in your organization today?
- What level of leadership is making those decisions?
- What kind of thinking is being used to make those decisions?
- How does it align with the **ROADD** model?
- What's your win/loss average?
- If you looked at the data by leadership level what would you discover?

Review the same data 6–12 months after you've introduced three or four organizational thinking tactics. We believe your before and after data will be mind-blowing!

And for those of you who are working at a company where your executive team doesn't have this idea on their radar—no worries. You don't have to wait for permission and/or round up executive support to incorporate these organizational thinking tactics into YOUR daily habits. You can put these organizational thinking tactics into practice on your own. And we can tell you this: You're not going to hurt the organization, diminish your department's results, or damage your professional reputation if you decide to help your team think more deeply! ☺

6

Organizational Thinking Tactic 1:

The Growth Questions

THINK

We shared The Growth Questions with you in a previous chapter. And ... The Growth Questions are worth repeating.

- **What worked?**
- **What didn't work?**
- **What will you do differently next time?**

When should you use The Growth Questions? Anytime—with one exception. You shouldn't use this tactic when an employee is not meeting expectations and you have already talked with them multiple times about correcting their behavior. That situation calls for a corrective action conversation—and there's a different model for that. This chapter is not the place nor time for that model. We would, however, be happy to share it with you. Grab it at https://info.becomemoregp.com/difficultconvo.

Other than that, we can't think of a time when these Growth Questions wouldn't be appropriate. For instance, we think you should ask these three questions after you or your staff …

- Presents an idea
- Addresses a conflict with a co-worker
- Tries out a new process
- Publicly disagrees with a leadership decision
- Gossips about another co-worker
- Makes a good decision
- Makes a bad decision
- Writes a report
- Blows a presentation
- Attends a workshop
- Turns in an assignment
- Trains a new co-worker
- Misses a deadline
- Travels for work
- Tries something for the first time
- Tries something for the 100th time

Please notice that we've included "under-performing" situations on this list. You can and should use The Growth Questions when people are learning. And as people learn, they're going to make mistakes. In fact, that is HOW they learn.

People often want to reject this idea. Organizations don't like failure. Individuals don't like failure. And ... Let's look at a very obvious example. Kids.

Children do not simply stand up and walk one day. There's a learning process. It starts with rolling over, then scooting, followed by crawling, then standing up and falling down —over and over again. Then, finally, taking their first step.

And what does every parent, grandparent, godparent, aunt and uncle, friend, neighbor, and even strangers do as this child goes through this learning curve? We encourage them. We goo and giggle at them. We smile and clap our hands when they try to stand up and end up falling on their bum instead. We even hold favored toys—just outside of their reach—to entice them to try.

Funny thing ... the process of trying, failing, recognizing how to do it better, receiving encouragement, and trying again ... works. And works well. Yet somehow, we've got it in our heads that we need to do things perfectly the first time. And this "need" for perfection is only increasing. A study published in Psychological Bulletin [48] found that college students who graduated in 2016—when compared to 1989 graduates—experienced more pressure to be perfect. The data shows:

- Self-imposed perfectionism score increased by 10%.
- Society imposed perfectionism score increased by 33%.
- Other imposed perfectionism score increased by 16%.

That's a pretty heavy burden to carry.

Organizations that use The Growth Questions establish a different standard. When you consistently and systematically ask The Growth Questions—over and over again—you proclaim that personal and professional development is essential. You reveal that growth is a process. You walk people through the learning curve associated with their new skill set. You encourage them to try, fail, learn from their "not-so-perfect" attempts, and try again. And you let them know that where they are today (What worked?) is good. AND that they are not done yet. No matter their level of experience, there is ALWAYS room to grow, expand, and become more. Even superstars can level up.

The Growth Questions also take the sting out of the development process. Think about the last time you received feedback. How did it go? Did you experience it as a positive or negative conversation? Did you agree with or reject the assessment? What did you do afterwards? Did you make any conscious changes? Did you grow?

In our experience, "getting feedback" is not something most people look forward to. Some folks SAY they want it. But many people have a difficult time staying in neutral, listening openly to a "critique," and not getting defensive. We've seen people react negatively to very small suggestions—like a few word changes in a report or a suggestion on how they might better utilize their time. And when people justify their decisions, they are not growing.

That's why we ask The Growth Questions in a very intentional order.

What Worked?
"What worked" must be the first question. When you start by emphasizing what's right, you

- Reduce defensiveness.
- Create a sense of accomplishment.
- Recognize contributions.
- Establish a supportive environment.
- Build morale.
- Increase psychological safety.
- Foster a sense of ownership and pride.

THINK

- Open the door for behavioral change.

And when you look at what's right—first—you're reinforcing positive behaviors and practices. Effectively you're saying, "You're doing this well, and I want you to continue doing it." [49] [50] [51] [52]

We'd also like you to note that the leader isn't telling their employee what worked. The leader is ASKING the employee what worked. When the employee answers first, it provides the leader an insight into what the employee knows. What their definition of success is. The breath of their perspective. And the depth of their contextual understanding. The leader needs to tuck this information away for future coaching opportunities. And in the moment, as soon as the employee finishes up with their list of "what worked," the boss needs to ADD to the list.

Imagine that for a minute. The employee is a little uncomfortable sharing what went well. They don't want to look like a braggart. So, they list two or three things that went well. Now the boss is teed up perfectly to add two or three more things to the list.

This is a great way for leaders to

- Convey that they really are paying attention.
- Specify how THIS individual adds value for the boss, the team, and the organization.
- Provide positive reinforcement.

All of which, by the way, are things that strengthen psychological safety, boost engagement, and increase retention.

And when you start with the good stuff, it establishes—up front—that the employee is not in trouble. You're NOT having a corrective action conversation. You're NOT hiding a hammer behind a veneer of niceness. You, as their leader, do NOT have an agenda, nor are you on a fault-finding mission. This conversation is about leveling up, continuous improvement, becoming more. And isn't that the whole point of feedback in the first place?

Honestly, we need to let you know that implementing this tactic might take a while. Staff is often skeptical. Their prior work history may have taught them to not trust leadership. YOUR previous policies and methodologies may have taught them to not trust YOU. AND, as the organization and individual leaders prove over time that employees will not experience any fallout from fully participating in The Growth Questions—the staff will become more open and honest with the process. And believe it or not, eventually employees then begin to candidly contribute when their leaders ask them the next two growth questions.

What Didn't Work?
We've been asking our staff this question for—well, for as long as we can remember. For the two of us, talking about what didn't work is normal. We're achievers by nature. That means we're seldom satisfied. And as soon as we have achieved something, we raise the bar.

With that said, sometimes the question "What didn't work?" doesn't spark the conversation we'd LIKE people to have. In many organizations, this question is used to lay blame, and/or identify scapegoats. Please don't ask "What didn't work?" in that way. Instead, ask it with the same honorable intentions that John Blakely demonstrates.

Who's John Blakely? Well, he is a successful trial lawyer who also happens to be Sara Blakely's father. If you don't know Sara, she founded Spanx®, the shapewear company that was valued at $1.2 billion in 2021. And Sara gives her father a lot of credit for her success.

You see, John created a weekly family ritual where he would ask his kids about their failures that week. They would then look for and discuss the "hidden gifts" inside these experiences. And finally, they would celebrate the missteps. By handling slip-ups this way, John took away failure's stigma and demonstrated that mistakes are part of life's journey. He showed them how reflecting on these small blunders can lead to invaluable insights. And he proved to them that these priceless perceptions could be the stepping-stones to growth, learning, and lifelong success. [53]

If you're going to make The Growth Questions work for you and your organization, YOU have to take the stigma out of making mistakes. How can you do that?

1. The employee needs to answer this question—not the boss.
2. It's OK if the employee doesn't list everything. They will get it when they get it.
3. It's best if the leader does NOT add additional What-Didn't-Work items to the employee's list.

What a leader CAN do is ask questions to ensure they understand why the employee thinks something didn't go well. And when an employee explains their thinking, we have found:

- **Sometimes what THEY think didn't go well, WE think did go well.** When this happens, it's the perfect time for the leader to say that THEY thought this item should have been on the "what worked" list—and then explain why they see it that way.

- **Sometimes the reason they think it didn't go well is NOT why it didn't go well.** When this happens, a good way for the leader to respond is to say something like, "I agree with you that it didn't work like you had hoped. I think, however, that the reason it didn't work might have been because ..."

In both cases it's important that the leader doesn't say, "You're wrong." Remember, growth is a journey, not a destination. And the goal is to level up. It's about taking one step in the right direction—not finishing the race. And we know that when we allow people to think things through and discover their own answers it shortens their learning curve and they grow FASTER! [54] [55]

It would also be wise to remember that no matter what, when a boss asks this question—it's scary! Employees are not used to admitting their mistakes. And more than likely, they have been reprimanded for making mistakes in the past. So, you need to be patient AND don't stop.

Since we've been asking these questions for years, we've learned it sometimes takes 6 to 18 months for a new employee to accept this process, tell their full truth during the process, and begin to learn and grow by using the process.

Yes, that's a long time. And it really comes down to

trust. Does this employee's previous work experience suggest that leaders are trustworthy? Has the organization (AND you as the leader) demonstrated that participating in The Growth Questions is safe? In other words, do we make employees feel safe during and after the process, or do they experience a "gotcha" moment? How is vulnerability perceived in the organization?

If your organization actions align with Brené Brown who believes that "vulnerability is not weakness; it's our greatest measure of courage," you can shorten this learning curve. If however, vulnerability is considered a fatal flaw ... this organizational thinking tactic probably won't work in your organization. [56]

What Will You Do Differently Next Time?
When you ask questions 1 and 2, you're looking for a list. When you get to question 3, you're asking the employee to make a choice and a commitment. You're basically saying, "Now that you've thought it through ... what's the one thing that you're willing to do differently?"

Why just ONE thing? Imagine for a minute that your significant other wanted to discuss ways to improve your relationship.

THINK

And by the end of the conversation, you had identified six things that would be helpful.

1. Listen.
2. Recognize when emotional support is needed.
3. Take on more of the household chores.
4. Work fewer hours and get home before 6 p.m.
5. Spend more time with the kids.
6. Go to bed together each night.

How would you feel if you were expected to do all six of those things right NOW?

Yes, maybe all six of those things would truly make a difference. And ... there's no need to pile on. The research is clear. It's easier, more sustainable, and actually faster when we focus on improving one thing at a time. [57] [58]

So, what's a leader to do when an employee is making a list of things they want to do differently instead of choosing one thing? Provide some clarity on what a good decision looks like.

For instance, you might say:

- To speed up the process next time, what will you do differently?
- To get a yes next time, what one thing will you do differently?
- To fix the quality issues, what will you do differently in the future?
- To get the biggest return on your effort, what will you do differently next time?

Notice that the first half of each question points at a specific outcome. The second part of the question asks what action will be done to achieve that specific outcome. And if an employee continues to want to do more than one thing, just ask them what they will do FIRST. ☺

7

Organizational Thinking Tactic 2:

Stay Stupid Longer

THINK

This is one of our favorites. And we've found that it's one of the hardest tactics to execute. Why? Because leaders, at every level, often believe that the primary way they add value is by having the answers. They think that they will have more authority and credibility when they can answer questions immediately. And they assume that their promotion opportunities improve when they demonstrate how smart they are.

And they are wrong.

We shared in our book Chief Optimization Officer that

THINK

these opinions are actually myths. [59]

Research demonstrates that leaders who

- ASK instead of TELL are more respected. [60]
- Talk less have better outcomes. [61]
- Purposefully don't answer employee questions end up with a staff that thinks for themselves, has a higher level of competence, and feels more empowered and motivated. [62] [63] [64]

Isn't that interesting? Many of us spend all of this time and energy trying to prove how smart we are, when the #1 reason leaders get promoted is by consistently delivering tangible results. And the best way to deliver tangible results is by having a TEAM that can effectively and efficiently get the work done. And the best way to develop a team that performs like that is to stay stupid longer. ☺

This makes sense—logically. However, in the heat of the moment, when there are deadlines that have to be hit, client and executive leader demands that need to be met, and a **Rodney** running around in our head insisting that we take action—NOW ... we end up just answering the question, solving the problem, and/or providing explicit instructions on what to do next.

Every single leader we know, including ourselves, gets caught in this trap. We inadvertently accept our staff's monkeys. [65]

So, what's the secret? What do we need to do differently to help us stay stupid longer?

We need to develop new leadership habits. And you know if you've read The Power of Habit by Charles Duhigg, you can modify your habits once you understand your triggers. Let's look at something that many of us do every day.

It's 3 o'clock in the afternoon. You've been at your desk, working hard since lunchtime. You're tired and your shoulders are a little tight from sitting in front of the computer for the last couple of hours. So, you head toward the breakroom, stop by Janique's office—which is on the way—for a quick chat, and eventually get to the breakroom. You grab an energy drink and a Snickers® bar, and head back to your office.

This is called your habit loop.

- **Your Trigger:** Leaving your office in the middle of the afternoon.
- **Your Typical Routine:** A friendly conversation capped off when you grab something to eat and drink from the vending machine.
- **Your Reward:** A change of pace, comradery, and/or satisfying your hunger and thirst.

THINK

Now—let's just say that you've realized that eating Snickers bars and guzzling energy drinks isn't doing you any good. So, you've decided it's time to break your 3 p.m. habit. You could go cold turkey and use sheer willpower to overcome your habit. Or you could keep the trigger and reward from your original habit loop and choose a healthier option for your routine—which could look something like ...

Your new habit loop.

- **Your Trigger:** Leaving your office in the middle of the afternoon.
- **Your New Routine:** A friendly conversation with Janique while you sip a can of sparkling water and munch on some crunchy carrots that you brought from home.
- **Your Improved Reward:** A change of pace, comradery, and a better, healthier way of satisfying your hunger and thirst.

Got it? Okay, let's apply this to staying stupid longer.

Your current habit loop.

- **Your Trigger:** An employee comes to your office and asks you a question.
- **Your Typical Routine:** You answer their question.

- **Your Reward:** They know what to do and they leave you in peace to finish your work. AND you feel good because you "helped."

Your new habit loop.

- **Your Trigger:** An employee comes to your office and asks you a question.
- **Your New Routine:** You ask them the four questions that you've written on a Post-It® note and stuck on your monitor.
  1. What's happening right now?
  2. What options have you considered?
  3. Which one do you think is best and why?
  4. What are you recommending that we do now?
- **Your Improved Reward:** Now that <u>they</u> have thought it through, <u>they</u> know what to do, not only today—but in the future. <u>Their</u> thinking leads to growth. (And the added benefit is that they'll leave you in peace to finish your work more and more often ☺).

Let's try this with another typical trigger.

Your current habit loop.

- **Your Trigger:** A weekly team meeting.
- **Your Typical Routine:** You sit at the head of the table. You lead the meeting. And you do the majority of the talking.

- **Your Reward:** It's easy. It's fast. And everyone hears the same information at the same time.

Your new habit loop.

- **Your Trigger:** Your weekly team meeting.
- **Your New Routine:** You make the decision that ALL of your one-way communication will be shared via email, team chat, or pre-recorded video messaging. When you hold team meetings it will be because you are looking for input and interaction, which means you will
    1. Sit anywhere BUT the head of the table.
    2. Assign agenda items to various members of your team and let them lead.
    3. Avoid making eye contact when people look to you for an answer, and when pushed you'll respond by saying something like, "I don't know, what do all of you think?"
    4. Keep track of the number of times you take over the meeting and what triggered you to do so. (This will help you learn how to stay stupid EVEN longer.)
- **Your Improved Reward:** Once you master this new routine it will make your life easier. When you stop holding informational meetings you'll save a ton of time. And with your team working together to discuss what they know,

THINK

identify options and alternatives, analyze their choices, and decide and execute (do) the next steps—you'll begin to see better results.

Staying stupid longer is HARD. Every bone in most leaders' bodies wants to make a decision, take action, and get it done. There's an **All-Knowing Alberto** hiding in almost all of us. AND—purposefully asking questions (instead of telling), limiting our airtime (instead of dominating the airtime), and choosing to NOT answer employee questions is a powerful way to encourage deeper thinking.

8

Organizational Thinking Tactic 3:

Readers Are Thinkers

THINK

Scott helped a client hire an HR executive a few years ago. Part of the contract included onboarding this new team member. And since we love Michael Watkins' book The First 90 Days, Scott used it as the foundation for their weekly coaching sessions.

After a couple of weeks, it became clear that this new hire was not reading the chapters that she had been assigned. When asked about it, she told Scott that reading was old-fashioned and that young professionals don't read.

Yikes. That might be her opinion. However, it is not accurate.

THINK

Let's look at what the data has to say ...

	Gen Z (Zoomers) 1997–2012	Millennials 1981–1996	Gen Xers 1965–1980	Boomers 1946–1964
Have read a book in the last 12 months	47%	80%	50%	70%
Consider themselves avid readers	27.1%	47.9%	50.7%	55.7%
Keep a list of books for future reading	44.6%	39.5%	36%	32.8%
Take advantage of public libraries	47.0%	39.5%	40.4%	36.6%
Prefer to read print books over audio books and e-books/tablets	Yes	Yes	Yes	Yes
Read e-books/tablets	31.7%	40.9%	35%	31.9%
Listen to audio books	19.4%	24%	18.5%	11.3%

People of all generations ARE reading. [66] In fact, right around 50% of ALL people, regardless of their age, consider themselves avid readers. Every generation prefers to have a good old-fashioned print book in their hands when they read. AND ... our Millennials and Gen Xers are more open to reading in formats other than print.

We know that the majority of your staff does read. So how can you leverage reading into an organizational advantage? Read with purpose. Just like going to the gym strengthens physical muscles, reading strengthens mental muscles. It's a workout for our brains. Decide which mental muscles you want to build, and then create opportunities for reading to build richer team-thinking skills. How does that work?

Reading Can Take Your Team to New Places
Think of reading as virtual reality for your team members' brains. By reading, they get to experience things they have not yet encountered. Consider what happens when your staff reads a non-fiction book. They have the opportunity to learn from experts, explore history, and dive into big ideas. It's like having a conversation with some of the smartest people in the world and talking about concepts that they might not have even considered previously.

Even if your team only wants to read fiction, they can experience walking in someone else's shoes. Feeling their emotions. Experiencing their world view. And believe it or not, reading fiction builds real-world empathy and emotional intelligence. [67] [68] Know anyone that could use a boost in that!?!?

Reading Can Help Your Team Become Super-Sleuths
When we read, our brains take over and we start analyzing everything. Who's the bad guy? What was the hidden meaning in that exchange? If that really happened, what would that suggest?

You see, we're actually practicing how to think more deeply when we analyze characters, follow arguments, look for clues, and do our best to discern what is true and what is not true. And all of this thinking can improve your team's real-life problem-solving skills as they learn to spot BS, think things through logically, and make smarter decisions.

Reading Can Improve Your Team's Focus
Got a "Dug the Dog" on your team? Who's Dug? You know—from Pixar's movie Up? [69] The character who is constantly distracted and shouts out "Squirrel!" as he runs off to chase a new thing. We love Dug—in the movie. And the Dugs at work drive most of us crazy.

Lots of people believe our ability to focus is just something we're born with. Not necessarily. While the ability to focus is a complex trait that is impacted by some innate predispositions, research in neuroscience, psychology, and cognitive science tells us that, with practice, we can improve our ability to focus.[70][71][72][73] In other words, the Dugs of our workplace are not destined to be constantly distractable.

Reading improves focus. It helps us keep our brains on track. And just like extending how far you can run, you can increase your focus by lengthening the number of pages you read in a sitting—a little bit at a time.

Reading Can Expand Your Team's Contextual Understanding

Oh, for a world that was simple and easy to understand. Wouldn't it be fantastic if there was a right and wrong answer for everything? But like we discussed in an earlier chapter—that's just not how the world works. And unfortunately, teaching staff how to recognize issues, pressures, constraints, and risks—skills associated with good decision making—is not something organizations have traditionally invested in. What companies often do is use all of that information to explain *why* they have made an unpopular decision.

You could choose to do this differently. What if your team read a book together that explored a between-a-rock-and-a-hard-place choice? What if you had a book discussion that explored the characters' options and alternatives? What if you asked about life's big questions—like what's REALLY important? When you can't get everything you want—what's on your "can't live without" list?

How does this apply to organizational decision making? Reading books that illustrate difficult and abstract concepts broadens perspectives, allows individuals to see and make connections, and ultimately helps them understand.

Reading Will Improve Your Team's Communication Skills

Really? Reading is going to help your team become better communicators?

Absolutely.

Vocabulary
As people read, they are exposed to a whole new set of words, including words that they don't hear in everyday conversation. That exposure expands their vocabulary and enables them to be more precise and nuanced—in both their speaking and writing. [74]

Grammar and Syntax
Reading reinforces correct grammar and syntax. It exposes the reader to properly constructed sentences and paragraphs, which means they are learning language and sentence structure, punctuation, and word order—all without having to memorize a whole bunch of rules like we were supposed to do in

THINK

third grade.[75] These are the skills that help us express ourselves more clearly.

Writing Style

As people are exposed to different writing styles and techniques, they learn how distinct authors organize their thoughts, use persuasive language, and craft compelling narratives.[76] By now you've noticed that in this book we have a unique way of expressing ourselves. It's our voice. And it represents Tammy and Scott.

Each member of your team can improve the clarity of their messages and develop their OWN voice, or recognize when to adjust their voice based on their audience (e.g. client vs. coworker or coworker vs. director). Simply by reading books written by different authors.

Comprehension and Listening

We're finishing up with our favorite benefit. Reading improves comprehension, and that translates to better listening.[77] Yep. We'll say it again. Readers are better listeners. Why? Because when a reader follows the intricate details of a murder mystery or solves the puzzles that their favorite hero encounters on a quest, they are seeking understanding. This translates into improved listening skills in the reader's everyday lives.

At BecomeMore Group we've gone all-in on reading.

New hires receive six books BEFORE they start (soon to be seven ☺).

- Chief Optimization Officer by Scott Burgmeyer and Tammy K. Rogers
- Trusted Advisor by David H. Maister, Charles H. Green, and Robert M. Galford
- Let's Get Real or Let's Not Play by Mahan Khalsa and Randy Illig
- The Science of Dream Teams by Mike Zani
- QBQ! By John G. Miller
- The Advantage by Patrick M. Lencioni

Every year our team reads together. In 2025 we're reading:

- Boundaries for Leaders by Henry Cloud
- The Success Paradox by Gary C. Cooper
- The Six Disciplines of Strategic Thinking by Michael D. Watkins
- The Growth Advantage by Bob Lisser
- Think by Scott Burgmeyer and Tammy K. Rogers
- High Conflict by Amanda Ripley

We host a book club called Leadership, Learning & Libations.

We believe Michael Puck when he says, "Every book you read is like a warrior in your army. The more you read, the stronger your army."

We want the BecomeMore crew to be stronger. So, we invite our friends, clients, partners, peers, and neighbors to read along with us. And then we meet every other month on a Zoom call as each of us shuts our doors, puts up our feet, grabs a drink, and passionately agrees, disagrees, and talks about how the book could impact us individually and organizationally.

Those two hours are invaluable! It's FREE! Want to join us? Register at:

https://www.becomemoregp.com/bookclub

Every leadership program we develop for our clients includes reading.
Organizations cannot grow beyond their leaders. Leadership thinking and talent is an organization's governor. So if an organization wants to grow, its leaders have to grow first. Reading is the fastest and most effective way to learn, grow, and deepen leaders' thinking.

THINK

We know that organizationally when people read it changes everything. From the culture to the way people think to how the staff responds to changes. Reading works. Period.

9

Organizational Thinking Tactic 4:

Carve Out Thinking Time

THINK

We talked in the introduction about the relentless barrage of emails, the endless meetings, and all of the "urgent" requests we receive. In this frenzied and chaotic environment, the idea of setting aside dedicated "thinking time" might seem like a luxury. A cute and quaint notion reserved for philosophers and academics. Honestly, we get it. And, the truth—it's not cute or quaint. It's crucial. And it's a powerful tactic that can drive innovation, improve decision-making, and ultimately lead to organizational success.

Just as "staying stupid longer" forces us to resist the urge to provide immediate answers, carving out

THINK

thinking time requires that we resist the urge to fill every moment with activity. It's about recognizing that true productivity isn't measured by the number of tasks completed, but by the quality of thought that informs those tasks to deliver outcomes.

Let's read that again. **Productivity isn't measured by the number of tasks completed, but by the quality of thought that informs those tasks to deliver outcomes.**

Drop the mic!

Many leaders, and indeed many employees, operate under the misguided assumption that constant activity equates to value. They believe that being "busy" is synonymous with being productive. They equate responding to emails in real time, or attending every meeting, as proof of their dedication. They fear that stepping away from the immediate, the tangible, will make them appear idle, disengaged, or even incompetent.

That is an extremely dangerous fallacy.

As we saw with the concept of "staying stupid longer," our assumptions about how we add value are often wrong. Research consistently demonstrates that

- **Reflection enhances decision-making:** Leaders who dedicate time to reflection make

better, more informed decisions. (That's why it's the first step in the **ROADD** process.)
- **Creativity thrives in solitude:** Innovation often emerges from periods of focused, uninterrupted thought.
- **Strategic thinking requires space:** Long-term planning and strategic vision necessitate the ability to step back and contemplate the big picture.

The pressure to be constantly "on" is immense. And the cost of neglecting thinking time is even greater. It leads to

- **Reactive decision-making:** Without time for reflection, decisions become knee-jerk reactions to immediate problems, rather than proactive tactics for long-term success.
- **Stifled innovation:** When there's no space for creative thought, new ideas and solutions are lost.
- **Burnout and decreased morale:** The constant pressure of "busy work" leads to exhaustion and disengagement.

So, how do we carve out thinking time in a world that is actively discouraging it? Here are just a couple of options to consider.

Prioritize and Schedule Thinking Time

We know. This sounds absolutely crazy. And, it works.

Let's say that right now, in your organization, leaders don't spend any time thinking. Everyone is busy. No problem. You can start small. Institute a standard operating procedure (SOP) for your leaders where they are expected to spend the first 15 minutes of their work day:

- **Reflecting** on what they know needs to be done that day.
- Identifying a minimum of three **Options** and alternatives for getting that work done.
- **Analyzing** the upsides and downsides of these options.
- **Deciding** what is going to be done, when it's going to be done, and who will be involved in getting it done.
- Committing to the decision—what it will take to own and **Do** the follow-through.

Now, before someone suggests that they don't have time to think for 15 minutes each and every day, you might want to consider that these 15 minutes represent less than 1% of a 40-hour work week (.625%, to be specific). And you need to make sure your leaders know that these 15 minutes are sacred. No meetings. No texting. No interruptions. No other work.

THINK

The only reason that these 15 minutes should be interrupted is if there's an emergency. And before you think you just got a "get-of-jail-free" card, let's define what an emergency is: Someone is dying and/or the building is on fire. ☺

OK ... Maybe your organization is a little more advanced. What if your leaders actually do take the time to think—occasionally. However, it seems like a lot of them end up using their thinking time to handle "more urgent" matters. When you find yourself in this situation, add on to the SOP suggested above. Ask your leaders to continue spending the first 15 minutes of each day thinking AND block off another hour on their calendar for thinking during the week. They can find a timeframe and routine that works for them. Maybe it's a full hour on Thursday. Maybe they will decide to finish up each day with 12 minutes of thinking time.

The organization does not need to dictate the "how." You do however need to enforce the "what." And just like before—this time is to be blocked off on the leader's calendar and treated as if it is sacred. No meetings. No texting. No requests from internal customers for this time. No other work.

Tammy blocks this time on her calendar with a TT. And the TT has two meanings: Tammy Time AND Thinking Time.

THINK

Finally, if your organization has been working on this for a while you may want to have a candid conversation with each leadership level. Get your supervisors together and discuss:

- The upside of setting aside thinking time.
- The purpose of thinking time.
- The kinds of things that would be beneficial to think about.
- How much thinking time they are using today.
- How much time they think they might need.

Repeat that conversation with your middle managers, directors/vice presidents, and executives. And then decide what systems, processes, and expectations your organization is going to develop around thinking time. And in case you're curious, if you ask AI about the "right" amount of time spent thinking, the computer-generated response would sound something like this:

While there is no definitive research on HOW MUCH time leaders should spend thinking, research does support the BENEFITS of thinking. And organizations should consider the quality of the thinking over the quantity of the thinking.

In addition, different levels of responsibility require different levels of thinking time. Middle managers are most often responsible for operational matters while executive leaders are responsible for strategy. So, a reasonable conclusion would be that middle managers spend 20% of their time thinking. And as a leader's responsibilities increase, so should their thinking time.

Host Thinking Retreats™
Sometimes we need to step away to step forward. That is what a Thinking Retreat is all about. It's a strategic intervention, a deliberate act of creating space for deep thought. And just like when we explored the power of carving out individual thinking time, Thinking Retreats extend this principle to the collective, fostering a shared time and space for focused reflection.

So, what exactly is a Thinking Retreat? It's a planned period, typically ranging from a half-day to several days, where a team or group of individuals step away from their usual work environment to engage in focused thinking. It's a deliberate break from the operational noise, a chance to disconnect from the "urgent," and an opportunity to reconnect with the "important."

How do Thinking Retreats work? The process is less about rigid agendas and more about creating a conducive environment for thought. This often involves

- **Physical Separation:** Moving away from the office, to a location that minimizes distractions.

- **Individual Exploration:** Time alone to grapple with individual thoughts, issues, and/or ideas/concepts.
- **Collaborative Exploration:** A professionally facilitated time that allows participants to share their thinking, brainstorm, collect diverse perspectives, gather ideas for overcoming roadblocks, and deepen their thinking.

The benefits of Thinking Retreats are profound. Thinking Retreats allow organizations to

- **Gain Strategic Clarity:** Stepping back from daily tasks enables a broader perspective, leading to more-informed strategic decisions.
- **Foster Innovation:** Uninterrupted time and space encourage creative thinking and the generation of new ideas.
- **Address Complex Issues:** Problems that cannot be solved in the office can be tackled with dedicated time.
- **Strengthen Team Cohesion:** Shared experiences and collaborative exploration strengthen team bonds and improve communication.
- **Reduce Burnout:** Providing a break from the usual pressure can revitalize teams and improve morale.

Cal Newport is the author of a book called Deep Work[78]. He makes the case that deep work, described as "professional activities performed in a state of distraction-free concentration," is the key to achieving meaningful organizational results. Thinking Retreats set the organization's leaders up to do deep work.

Promote Slow Thinking
Yep. We know. That's CRAZY. We might as well be suggesting you throw the baby out with the bath water.

Consider all of the **Echo Chamber Evelyns, Terry the Trend Followers, Sound Bite Steves, All-Knowing Albertos, Jumping Julias,** and **Running Rodneys** in your organization. How many of them are making hasty judgements, have quick trigger reactions, and are ultimately generating less-than-optimal outcomes?

OK. We COULD just blame this on your staff. But step back a minute and contemplate how your organization reinforces the need for speed. For instance, would people describe your organization as having

- An "always on" mentality.
- A 24/7 expectation.
- Performance metrics that emphasize and prioritize speed.
- Preference for quick thinkers.

- A culture that rewards "fire fighters."
- Meetings where people are expected to contribute on the spot.
- Rules about the time allowed between receiving and responding to emails.
- A performance management system that incentivizes quickness.

Yes, service and production expectations make sense. They, however, are often misunderstood, and when carried out to the nth degree, they can lead to trouble. So, we suggest combining these kinds of expectations with a "slow thinking" twist.

What do we mean by that? "Slow thinking" is the deliberate choice of resisting the urge to take immediate action. Instead, encourage employees to pause, reflect, identify options, and analyze those options BEFORE they make a decision.

Yep, that's the **ROADD** model.

Using **ROADD** doesn't have to take an hour, half-a-day, or a week. Once people get the hang of it ... in many situations, employees can be completely down the **ROADD** in less than a couple of minutes.

And what could those couple of minutes buy you? Here are some examples we have found:

- A decrease in customer escalations.
- A smaller number of emails sent in ALL CAPS.

- Reduced rework.
- Co-workers who ask instead of assuming.
- Fewer jerks at work.
- Improved collaboration and cooperation.
- Increased engagement.
- Better results.

Yes. Sometimes it's wiser to go slow-slow instead of going quick-quick. And since going slower actually benefits the organization, it's critical that the organization helps its employees make this distinction.

Build Thinking Sanctuaries
In 2020 corporations sent everyone home to work. In 2025, they're asking everyone to come back to work. And, let's face it. This is not the easiest or most popular transition. And yet—even in the midst of this tumultuous shift—we're still recommending that organizations make another workplace modification. We would like you to consider creating Thinking Sanctuaries.

Many of our white-collar clients have open-office floor plans. And yes, open offices connect us to one another. In this kind of space, we can simply raise our voices a little bit and ask our neighbor across the half-wall for their perspective. And we can certainly keep a tab on our culture and ensure we're acting like the company we want to be.

THINK

All of that is true, AND ... the need for focused, uninterrupted thought has never been greater.

That's why we need Thinking Sanctuaries. Thinking Sanctuaries are not simply empty rooms. They are intentionally designed spaces that are carefully crafted to minimize distractions and promote contemplation. And they could look like ...

- **Dedicated Rooms:** Soundproofed rooms with comfortable seating, soft lighting, and minimal visual stimuli.
- **Library-Style Spaces:** Areas with individual workstations, noise-canceling headphones, and access to research materials.
- **Nature-Inspired Zones:** Spaces with natural light, plants, and calming water features, promoting a sense of tranquility.
- **Meditation or Mindfulness Rooms:** Rooms designed for guided or independent meditation, with comfortable cushions and calming ambiance.
- **Enclosed Booths:** Individual, small spaces, that allow for personal quiet time.

The benefits of these quiet spaces are profound. They allow employees to ...

- **Enhance Focus and Concentration:** By minimizing distractions, these spaces enable deeper engagement with complex tasks.

- **Improve Cognitive Function:** Studies have shown that quiet environments can reduce stress and improve cognitive performance. [79]
- **Foster Creativity and Innovation:** Uninterrupted time and space allow for more creative problem-solving and idea generation.
- **Reduce Stress and Burnout:** Providing a sanctuary from the constant stimulation of the workplace can promote relaxation and reduce stress.
- **Promote Deeper Thinking:** These spaces facilitate the kind of contemplative thought that leads to strategic insights and informed decisions.

Organizations can implement these spaces by ...

- **Conducting Needs Assessments:** Survey employees to understand their preferences and needs for quiet spaces.
- **Designing Intentional Spaces:** Collaborate with designers to create spaces that are both functional and aesthetically pleasing.
- **Establishing Clear Guidelines:** Set rules for use, such as noise levels and time limits, to ensure that the spaces remain conducive to quiet thought.
- **Promoting Awareness and Accessibility:** Communicate the availability and benefits of quiet spaces to employees.

- **Leading by Example:** Leaders should demonstrate their own use of quiet spaces, reinforcing their value.

And when organizations invest in Thinking Sanctuaries, they are communicating that deep thinking is NOT a luxury, it is an organizational expectation.

10

Organizational Thinking Tactic 5:

Expand Facilitation & Problem Solving

THINK

We've all sat in meetings where the leader asks a question and waits for someone to answer. Eventually someone, either a **Get Along Gary** or the individual with the least amount of patience, answers. This facilitative technique is called a "shout out." You shout out a question to the entire group and anyone and everyone is invited to answer.

It's just one of many facilitation techniques that get people to participate. It is however some leaders' ONLY facilitative technique. And that's a shame.

Shout outs favor extroverts. Shout outs encourage one-and-done thinking. Shout outs reinforce shallow thinking.

If an organization wants to cultivate a culture of deeper thinking, they need to use a wide variety of facilitation techniques that encourage individuals to reflect, consider, contemplate, interact, and analyze—not just react. Some of the most familiar facilitation tools and methodologies that are used in continuous improvement include:

- Affinity Diagrams
- 5W1H
- Fishbone
- Multi-Voting
- Observation Data Collection
- Plus/Minus

And if you're more familiar with workshops and training sessions, maybe these facilitation methodologies will ring a bell:

- Post-It Note Brainstorming
- Hot Dots
- Fist of Five
- Mind Mapping
- Gallery Walks
- Journaling
- Think, Pair, Share
- If That, Then

We are not going to take the time in this book to walk you through these exercises and explain how to use them. We have already published three books that describe a host of continuous improvement tools and their implementation. And more than likely we'll soon write a book to introduce our favorite training and development facilitative methodologies.

In the meantime, to help your organization expand and incorporate additional facilitative tools, you may want to consider sending some of your leaders to a DMAIC WAY® Green Belt course and/or our Extreme Facilitation™ workshop.

These are our two most popular public workshops. And while we know this sounds like a sales pitch (which of course, it is), what makes a BecomeMore workshop better and more effective is our facilitation skills. And we made the decision years ago that instead of keeping this transformational skill set to ourselves—we'd help organizations bring these facilitative skills in house.

We host four Extreme Facilitation workshops a year. And since the class is limited to six participants it means that 24 people have the privilege of learning and practicing master facilitation techniques with us each year. There are a few more seats in our Green Belt course. And if your organization truly wants to embed deeper thinking and facilitation skills into your culture, The DMAIC Way is truly a course and certification you should consider. You can find all these workshops on our website at

THINK

https://www.becomemoregp.com/workshops.

Facilitation and problem solving aren't just nice-to-have skills—they're essential tactics for driving meaningful thinking and the ability to implement sustainable improvement.

Organizations that invest in facilitation and problem solving are investing in their people's ability to think critically, communicate effectively, and work collaboratively. These skills aren't optional in a high-performing culture; they're foundational. Whether it's through DMAIC Way or Extreme Facilitation or other means, developing these capabilities means you're not just improving processes—you're transforming the way people work together.

11

Organizational Thinking Tactic 6:

Lead Them Down the ROADD

THINK

By this point in the book, you know what the **ROADD** model is. We hope you've Reflected about how it could transform your work and your team. You may have thought about some Options for incorporating it. (Turn it over to your internal training team? Give everyone in the organization a copy of this book? Invite us to facilitate workshops for your staff?) As you Analyze those and any other options, we suggest that the best way for your organization to incorporate the **ROADD** model into your culture is to put it in action (aka Decide and Do).

Simply make it part of your team's daily routine. And there's a very easy way that your leaders can do that.

THINK

It's just a matter of asking the right question at the right time. To help you, we've created a guide with examples that your leaders can follow to ensure they are asking GREAT questions all the time. All leaders have to do is identify where on the **ROADD** their employee is and pick questions that best fit the situation.

ROADD Questions

REFLECT

- What's happening right now?
- What else do you know about this situation?
- What does success look like?
- What are your current assumptions about this situation?
- How are your past experiences influencing your perspective?
- What biases might be affecting your thinking?
- What do you actually know versus what you think you know?
- What are your cognitive strengths and weaknesses in this type of situation?
- Who else might have insights and an objective point of view?

OPTIONS

- What's the standard way of handling this kind of situation?
- What other options have you considered?
- What else can you think of?
- Build on that idea for a while.
- What would be a completely unconventional approach?
- What might be considered a counter-proposal?
- Who else could you talk with that might have a different point of view?
- What options exist that we haven't considered yet?
- How could we break out of our typical thought patterns to identify new possibilities?

ANALYZE

- Which of your options do you feel the most confident about right now?
- Let's start with your first one. What do you think will be the upside? Downside? Risks?
- What data and/or evidence supports your point of view?
- How reliable is your data and/or evidence?
- What impact will this option have on the rest of the organization?
- What might be the short-term consequences? Long-term consequences?

Repeat the above questions with at least 2 other options, then ...

- Compare and contrast your options.
- Ask which one has the biggest return on investment and consequences you can live with.

DECIDE

- Are you ready to make your decision?
- What would be the consequence of NOT making a decision today?
- Based on your analysis, what do you believe is the best course of action?
- Walk me through your thinking again.
- Are you willing to own this decision?
- Are you prepared to deal with and manage the downside of this decision?

DO

- Who needs to know about this decision?
- What specific steps will need to be taken to implement this decision?
- Who and what resources will you need to get this done?
- Who will be responsible for each step?
- What will the deadlines be for each step?
- How will you be able to monitor progress?
- What potential obstacles might you encounter?
- What will you do to prepare for them?
- How will you communicate this decision and the rollout plan to the various stakeholders?
- When will it be done?
- How will we know that this was a successful decision and that it's done-done?

The next time one of your leaders or team members shows up with shortcut thinking—acting like **Echo Chamber Evelyn** or **Get Along Gary** or any of their other shallow-thinking colleagues—you can turn to this model. It will help your team slow down, engage in deeper thinking, and get better results.

You can download the **ROADD** questions at: https://www.becomemoregp.com/thinktools

Conclusion

In Chapter 3 we introduced you to Ascend. And here's the rest of the story ...

In the first three years we worked with Amelia and Ascend we talked about all six of these organizational thinking tactics:

1. The Growth Questions
2. Staying Stupid Longer
3. Readers are Thinkers
4. Carving out Thinking Time
5. Expanding Facilitation and Problem Solving
6. Implementing the **ROADD** model

And believe us, Amelia didn't swallow our recommendations hook, link, and sinker. She challenged our thinking. She pushed back. And we all learned and grew through these conversations. Eventually, Amelia made some important decisions.

Year One

In year one, Amelia decided to implement just ONE tactic. She wanted to focus the organization and do ONE thing that she believed would have the biggest impact in the way her staff went about their work. And, she decided to NOT turn THINKING into a big organizational initiative. Instead, she made the decision to introduce this tactic to her senior team, and then reinforced it in staff meetings, 1:1s, and during casual conversations—like when she was walking down the hall with staff.

Which organizational thinking tactic did she start with? The Growth Questions.

After just a couple of months, Amelia's choice paid off. Not only was SHE asking her staff what worked, what didn't work, and what could they do differently. ALL of her senior leaders had started to ask THEIR staff The Growth Questions.

Interestingly enough, during this soft launch, Amelia discovered that The Growth Questions didn't work very well if SHE didn't Stay Stupid Longer. Which meant that Amelia ended up launching two organizational thinking tactics within days of one another. And that led to some pretty important coaching with her senior team.

Helping her team Stay Stupid Longer took some time—as well as more than a little pushing. It's hard to let go of having the answers. Some of Amelia's senior leaders' identities were tied to being the smart one that solved the tough problems and saved the day. And asking them to SSL not only didn't make sense to them—it felt like she was asking them to run a marathon without legs. One of Amelia's executive leaders told us that she was "throwing away the organization's MOST valuable asset."

Yes, AND ... Staying Stupid Longer builds value as staff members learn to think, take action, and solve problems independently. And most of the senior team eventually discovered that the organization wasn't losing assets when they stayed stupid longer—they were significantly <u>multiplying</u> the organization's assets.

As Amelia watched these two tactics cascade through the organization, she realized that the structured process of thinking that we had talked with her about would provide her team with a linear and logical framework to follow. So, in month four, she started walking her senior team down the **ROADD** model in their problem-solving meetings.

And let's just say, Ameila's team embraced the **ROADD** model almost immediately. They liked the model's simplicity. They thought it was easy to remember, talk through, and execute. And, when they walked down the **ROADD** with their staff, they immediately saw how it expanded their staff's understanding and perspectives—as well as improved their thinking. The **ROADD** model was a hit!

So, what impact did Amelia's decisions have? You might remember from Chapter 3 that Amelia was concerned about her team bringing the same set of solutions to Ascend's customers. Twelve months after implementing these three organizational thinking tactics, Ascend's consultants were suggesting 30% more innovative solutions to their clients than they had the year before.

Yahoo! Ascend no longer had a bunch of **Running Rodneys**.

Year Two
With a win under her belt, Amelia decided to introduce a new organizational thinking tactic in year two. Her choice? Carve Out Thinking Time. This time, however, Amelia decided to formalize her expectations. At the beginning of the year, she announced a new policy. Every staff member was asked to block out two to four hours a week for thinking time.

Along with this new policy, Amelia decided that SHE needed to start modeling Slow Thinking. You see, Amelia knew that she had a reputation for jumping into the fray any time there were organizational forest fires. She also understood that she had a tendency to dominate organizational decision-making. That meant that Amelia was both a **Jumping Julia** AND an **All-Knowing Alberto**. Yikes. And she knew that if she wanted her team to think more deeply, she would need to lead the way.

Amelia made the decision that any time an urgent organizational issue popped up, she was going to resist the temptation to take immediate action. Instead, she was going to slow down, mosey along the **ROADD**, and bring her senior team along for the journey. And hopefully, not only would this reinforce the messages from year one, it would also expand her team's thinking and provide them with a bigger and broader conceptual understanding of what a good decision looks like.

The result? By the end of year two, recurring client issues had decreased by 40%.

Year Three
After 24 months, the questions we all began to ask were, "Is this sustainable?" and "Can we continue to shatter the status quo AND ensure that our Year One and Year Two successes will stick?"

THINK

With some additional deep thinking, ☺ Amelia decided to Build Thinking Sanctuaries to encourage her staff to read. Quarterly book clubs were established. Quiet corners were outfitted with comfy chairs. One of Ascend's conference rooms was transformed into a reading library. And small tables with chairs were installed throughout Ascend's outdoor areas.

Then an interesting thing happened. Folks began having conversations in cozy corners. People would check out books and spend their lunch hours reading in the sun outdoors. Amelia even started to see people sitting in their offices, feet up on their desks, deep in thought.

Yep, the place was quieter. And yet, you could feel the energy. The staff still talked about their kids, and who won the game. And, we noticed that their conversations were more substantive. They were talking less about people and more about ideas and concepts. We stopped hearing how it was done last time. Instead, people were discussing options and alternatives. And to be honest, we simply heard MORE people talking. Not just the dominant personalities. Even Ascend's introverts were contributing.

These changes in the culture were subtle and significant. What people read about, think about, and talk about makes a huge difference. Focusing on what CAN be done creates a culture of possibilities. And the more a team believes they CAN, the more they actually accomplish. [80] [81]

So, what were Ascend's results at the three-year mark? Amelia was pretty happy—and so was her board. Profitability had increased by 28%.

Lessons Learned
We're proud of the work we did with Ascend. We're prouder still of the work that Amelia and her team did. THEY did the work. THEY changed their habits and behaviors. THEY are reaping the rewards.

Ascend's journey demonstrates the impact of investing in organizational thinking. It's not just about teaching employees new skills; it's about creating a culture that fosters deep thinking, encourages collaboration, and embraces continuous improvement. Ascend's success proves that by prioritizing intellectual development, organizations can unlock their full potential, achieve a sustainable competitive advantage, and drive significant financial results. Investing in organizational thinking may come with a cost—AND, it can also be a powerful engine for growth and transformation!

Power Through the Discomfort of Change
You and your organization can transform your thinking. It's just a matter of determining what thinking tactics will work best for you.

1. The Growth Questions
2. Staying Stupid Longer
3. Reading
4. Carving Out Thinking Time
5. Embracing Facilitation & Problem Solving
6. Leading Them Down the **ROADD**

As you embrace one of these tactics, it's going to feel uncomfortable—at first.

Leaders won't know what to do with their thinking time. Staff will wonder why the way you conduct meetings has changed. And those sanctuaries ... You might discover that they're the most popular seats in the house.

As you walk this **ROADD**, remind yourself and your leaders not to feel guilty about not being "productive" when they are thinking. Watch as your staff becomes more and more involved and engaged. Pay close attention to what people are talking about. And look at where decisions are being made, and the outcomes of those decisions. Why? Because we know that over time, when you embed these tactics into your daily routines, you will reap the rewards of deeper organizational thinking.

References

1. Gartner. (n.d.). Reduce the staggering costs of poor operational decisions. Smarter with Gartner. Retrieved from https://www.gartner.com/smarterwithgartner/reduce-the-staggering-costs-of-poor-operational-decisions

2. Oncken, W., Jr., & Wass, D. L. (1974). Management time: Who's got the monkey? Harvard Business Review.

3. Robert K. Greenleaf Center for Servant Leadership. (n.d.). What is servant leadership? Retrieved April 4, 2025, from https://www.greenleaf.org/what-is-servant-leadership/

4. Mankins, M. C., & Garton, E. (2017). Time, talent, energy: Overcome organizational drag and unleash your team's productive power. Harvard Business Review Press.

5. Reclaim.ai. (n.d.). Setting priorities report: Top work challenges (50 stats).

6. Slingshot. (n.d.). Survey: 34% of workers have to guess their priorities at work.

7. Feldman, S. and Sherman, C. (2001) The High Cost of Not Finding Information: An IDC White Paper. IDC. https://www.scirp.org/reference/referencespapers?referenceid=1840731

8. Schubmehl, D. and Vesset D. (2014, June). The knowledge quotient: Unlocking the hidden value of information using search & content analytics. https://pages.coveo.com/rs/coveo/images/IDC-Coveo-white-paper-248821.pdf

9. Open Journal of Business and Management (2015). 3, 446-452 Published Online October 2015 in SciRes. http://www.scirp.org/journal/ojbm http://dx.doi.org/10.4236/ojbm.2015.34045

10. Jia, J., & Yin, Y. (2015). Analysis of Nokia's decline from marketing perspective. Open Journal of Business and Management, 3, 446-452. http://dx.doi.org/10.4236/ojbm.2015.34045

11. Stanford Technology Ventures Program. (2010, February 24). How did the AOL-Time Warner merger go wrong? https://stvp.stanford.edu/clips/how-did-the-aol-time-warner-merger-go-wrong/

12. Randolph, M. (2022, May 4). We pitched Netflix to Blockbuster. They laughed us out of the building. Built In. Retrieved April 4, 2025, from https://builtin.com/articles/netflix-blockbuster-buyout

13. Fiegerman, S. (2018, July 24). How Netflix beat its rivals and survived the 2000s. CNN Business. https://money.cnn.com/2018/07/24/technology/netflix-2000s/index.html

14. Forsdick, S. (2024, March 1). Blockbuster's former CEO on competition with Netflix and how to handle criticism. Raconteur. Retrieved April 4, 2025, from https://www.raconteur.net/leadership/blockbusters-ceo-james-keyes-netflix-competition

15. Product Development and Management Association.

16. Journal of Product Innovation Management.

17. National Transportation Safety Board. (n.d.). Monthly aviation dashboard.

https://www.ntsb.gov/safety/data/Pages/monthly-dashboard.aspx

18. Federal Aviation Administration. (n.d.). Air traffic by the numbers. https://www.faa.gov/air_traffic/by_the_numbers

19. Keillor, G. (1974–2016). News from Lake Wobegon [Radio segment]. A Prairie Home Companion.

20. Bar-Eli, M., Azar, O. H., Ritov, I., Keidar-Levin, Y., & Schein, G. (2007). Action bias among elite soccer goalkeepers: The case of penalty kicks. Journal of Economic Psychology, 28(5), 606-621. https://doi.org/10.1016/j.joep.2006.12.001

21. Butler, H. A. (2012). Halpern Critical Thinking Assessment and real-world outcomes: Cross-sectional analyses using national data. Thinking Skills and Creativity, 7(2), 112-121.

22. Moon, J. A. (2004). A Handbook of Reflective and Experiential Learning: Theory and Practice. London: Routledge Falmer. and Sandars, J. (2009). The use of reflection in medical education: AMEE Guide No. 44. Medical teacher, 31(8), 685-695.

23. Tanner, K. D. (2012). Promoting student metacognition. CBE—Life Sciences Education, 11(2), 113-120.

24. Flavell, J. H. (1979). Metacognition and cognitive monitoring: A new area of cognitive-developmental inquiry. American psychologist, 34(10), 906.

25. Eurich, T. (2018). *Insight: Why we're not as self-aware as we think, and how better self-knowledge empowers us for success*. Currency.

26. Guilford, J. P. (1967). The nature of human intelligence. McGraw-Hill.

27. Ericsson, K. A., Krampe, R. T., & Tesch-Römer, C. (1993). The role of deliberate practice in the acquisition of expert performance. Psychological review, 100(3), 363.

28. Burton & Bonanno, 2016; Kashdan, Barrios, Forsyth, & Steger, 2006; Kashdan & Rottenberg, 2010; Kashdan et al., 2006.

29. Schoemaker, P. J. (1995). Scenario planning: a tool for strategic thinking. Sloan management review, 36(2), 25-40.

30. Bandura, A. (1997). Self-efficacy: The exercise of control. W. H. Freeman and Company.

31. Thaler, R. H., & Sunstein, C. R. (2008). Nudge: Improving decisions about health, wealth, and happiness. Yale University Press.

32. Burke, L. E., Wang, J., & Sevick, M. A. (2011). Self-monitoring in weight loss: A systematic review of the literature. Journal of the Academy of Nutrition and Dietetics, 111(1), 92-102.

33. Davenport, T., and Harris, J. G. (2017, September 19). Competing on the analytics: The new science of winning. Harvard Business Review.

34. Kahneman, D. (2011). Thinking, fast and slow. Farrar, Straus and Giroux.

35. Pennycook, G., & Rand, D. G. (2019). Lazy, not biased: Susceptibility to partisan fake news is better explained by lack of reasoning than by motivated reasoning.

Cognition, 188, 39-50.
https://doi.org/10.1016/j.cognition.2018.06.011

36. von Neumann, J., & Morgenstern, O. (1944). Theory of games and economic behavior. Princeton University Press.

37. Kahneman, D., & Tversky, A. (2013). Prospect theory: An analysis of decision under risk. In Handbook of the fundamentals of financial decision making: Part I (pp. 99-127).

38. Hubbard, G. (2009). Measuring organizational performance: Beyond the triple bottom line. Business Strategy and the Environment, 18, 177-191. https://doi.org/10.1002/bse.564

39. Keeney, R. L., & Raiffa, H. (1976). Decisions with multiple objectives: Preferences and value tradeoffs. Cambridge University Press.

40. Bloom, B. S. (Ed.). (1956). Taxonomy of educational objectives: The classification of educational goals. Longmans, Green.

41. Helsdingen, A., van Gog, T., & van Merriënboer, J. (2011). The effects of practice schedule and critical thinking prompts on learning and transfer of a complex judgment task. Journal of Educational Psychology, 103(2), 383-398. https://doi.org/10.1037/a0022370

42. Gollwitzer, P. M. (1999). Implementation intentions: Strong effects of simple plans. American Psychologist, 54(7), 493.

43. Bandura, A. (1997). Self-efficacy: The exercise of control. W. H. Freeman and Company.

44. Fixsen, D. L., Naoom, S. F., Blase, K. A., Friedman, R. M., & Wallace, F. (2005). Implementation research: A synthesis of the literature. University of South Florida, Louis de la Parte Florida Mental Health Institute, National Implementation Research Network (NIRN).

45. Weick, K. E. (1984). Small wins: Redefining the scale of social problems. American Psychologist, 39(1), 40.

46. Imai, M. (1986). Kaizen: The key to Japan's competitive success. McGraw-Hill/Irwin.

47. Edmondson, A. C. (2018). The fearless organization: Creating psychological safety in the workplace for learning, innovation, and growth. John Wiley & Sons.

48. Curran, T., & Hill, A. (2017, December 28). Perfectionism is increasing over time: A meta-analysis of birth cohort differences from 1989 to 2016. Psychological Bulletin.

49. Seligman, M. E. P., & Csikszentmihalyi, M. (2000). Positive psychology: An introduction. American Psychologist, 55(1), 5-14.

50. Cooperrider, D. L., & Whitney, D. (2005). Appreciative inquiry: Collaborating for change. Berrett-Koehler Publishers.

51. Kluger, A. N., & DeNisi, A. (1996). The effects of feedback interventions on performance: A historical review, a meta-analysis, and a preliminary feedback intervention theory. Psychological Bulletin, 119(2), 254.

52. Argyris, C., & Schön, D. A. (1978). Organizational learning: A theory of action perspective. Addison-Wesley.

53. National CIO Review. (n.d.). Sara Blakely—Overcoming fear of failure. https://nationalcioreview.com/video/sara-blakely-overcoming-fear-of-failure/

54. Piaget, J. (1970). Genetic epistemology. Columbia University Press.

55. Vygotsky, L. S. (1978). Mind in society: The development of higher psychological processes. Harvard University Press.

56. Brown, B. (2015). Rising strong: The reckoning. The rumble. The revolution. Spiegel & Grau.

57. Clear, J. (2018). Atomic habits: An easy & proven way to build good habits & break bad ones. Avery.

58. Duhigg, C. (2012). The power of habit: Why we do what we do in life and business. Random House.

59. Burgmeyer, S., & Rogers, T. K. (2022). Chief optimization officer: Shattering the status quo. Happy Jack Publishing, LLC.

60. Gino, F. (2018). The business case for curiosity. Harvard Business Review, 96(5), 114-123.

61. Tost, L. P., Gino, F., & Larrick, R. P. (2013). When power makes others speechless: The negative impact of power on information exchange in dyads. Academy of Management Journal, 56(5), 1465-1484.

62. Deci, E. L., & Ryan, R. M. (2000). The "what" and "why" of goal pursuits: Human needs and the self-determination of behavior. Psychological Inquiry, 11(4), 227-268.

63. Spreitzer, G. M. (1995). Psychological empowerment in the workplace: Dimensions, measurement, and validation. Academy of Management Journal, 38(5), 1442-1465.

64. Knowles, M. S. (1980). The modern practice of adult education: From pedagogy to andragogy. Cambridge Adult Education.

65. Oncken, W., Jr., & Wass, D. L. (1974). Management time: Who's got the monkey? Harvard Business Review.

66. Albanese, A. R. (2019, July 17). Reading through the ages: Generational reading survey. Library Journal. https://www.libraryjournal.com/story/Reading-Through-the-Ages-Generational-Reading-Survey

67. Tamir, D. I., Bricker, A. B., Dodell-Feder, D., & Mitchell, J. P. (2016). Reading fiction and reading minds: The role of simulation in the default network. Social Cognitive and Affective Neuroscience, 11(2), 215-224. https://doi.org/10.1093/scan/nsv114

68. Bal, P. M., & Veltkamp, M. (2013). How does fiction reading influence empathy? An experimental investigation on the role of emotional transportation. PLOS ONE, 8(1), e55341. https://doi.org/10.1371/journal.pone.0055341

69. Docter, P. (Director). (2009). Up [Film]. Walt Disney Pictures; Pixar Animation Studios.

70. Davidson, R. J., & Dahl, C. J. (2018). Affective neuroscience: Past, present, and future. In Handbook of affective sciences (pp. 53-73). Oxford University Press.

71. Klingberg, T., Forssberg, H., & Westerberg, H. (2002). Training of working memory in children with ADHD. Journal of Clinical and Experimental Neuropsychology, 24(6), 781-791.

72. Pascual-Leone, A., Amedi, A., Fregni, F., & Merabet, L. B. (2005). The plastic human brain cortex. Annual Review of Neuroscience, 28, 227-268.

73. Rosen, L. D. (2012). iDisorder: Understanding our obsession with technology and overcoming its hold on us. Palgrave Macmillan.

74. Stanovich, K. E. (2000). Progress in understanding reading: Scientific foundations and new frontiers. Guilford Press.

75. Biber, D., Johansson, S., Leech, G., Conrad, S., & Finegan, E. (1999). Longman grammar of spoken and written English. Longman.

76. Pinker, S. (2014). The sense of style: The thinking person's guide to writing in the 21st century. Penguin Books.

77. Perfetti, C. A. (2007). Reading ability: Lexical quality to comprehension. Scientific Studies of Reading, 11(4), 357-383

78. Newport, C. (2016). Deep work: Rules for focused success in a distracted world. Grand Central Publishing.

79. Lercher, P., Evans, G. W., & Meis, M. (2003). Ambient noise and cognitive performance: The moderating effects of noise type. Journal of Environmental Psychology, 23(2), 175-181.

80. Bandura, A. (1997). Self-efficacy: The exercise of control. W. H. Freeman and Company.

81. Chen, G., Kirkman, B. L., Kanfer, R., Allen, D., & Rosen, B. (2007). Boosting motivation in teams: An examination of the interaction between regulatory focus and collective efficacy. Journal of Applied Psychology, 92(4), 1083-1092.

ABOUT THE AUTHORS

Scott Burgmeyer is the Founder and co-CEO of The BecomeMore Group. For more than 30 years, he has worked and consulted in virtually all industries, including manufacturing, laboratory, technology, education, and health care. He held roles such as Forensic Chemist, QA Director, CI Manager, Organizational Development, HR, SVP Quality & Improvement, Chief Improvement Officer and CEO.

Scott is a lifelong learner, professor, speaker, and author of multiple books, articles, and journal publications. As a Master Black Belt and creator of The DMAIC Way®, his goal is for everyone to Make it Better! Make it Stick!

Tammy K. Rogers began her career at a startup company in Minneapolis, designing employee satisfaction surveys. Within 6 months, she was tapped to lead the new training and development division.

Tammy has written more than 50 internationally distributed training programs and worked with best-selling authors like James Autry and Bob Nelson. In 1995, Tammy ventured out on her own, founding three organizations and today is Founder and co-CEO of The BecomeMore Group. Tammy is best known for advising leaders and organizations to become more by developing new ways of thinking, new attitudes, and new behaviors that translate into measurable results.

Made in the USA
Monee, IL
20 May 2025

17827186R00115